Spiyt th'Words

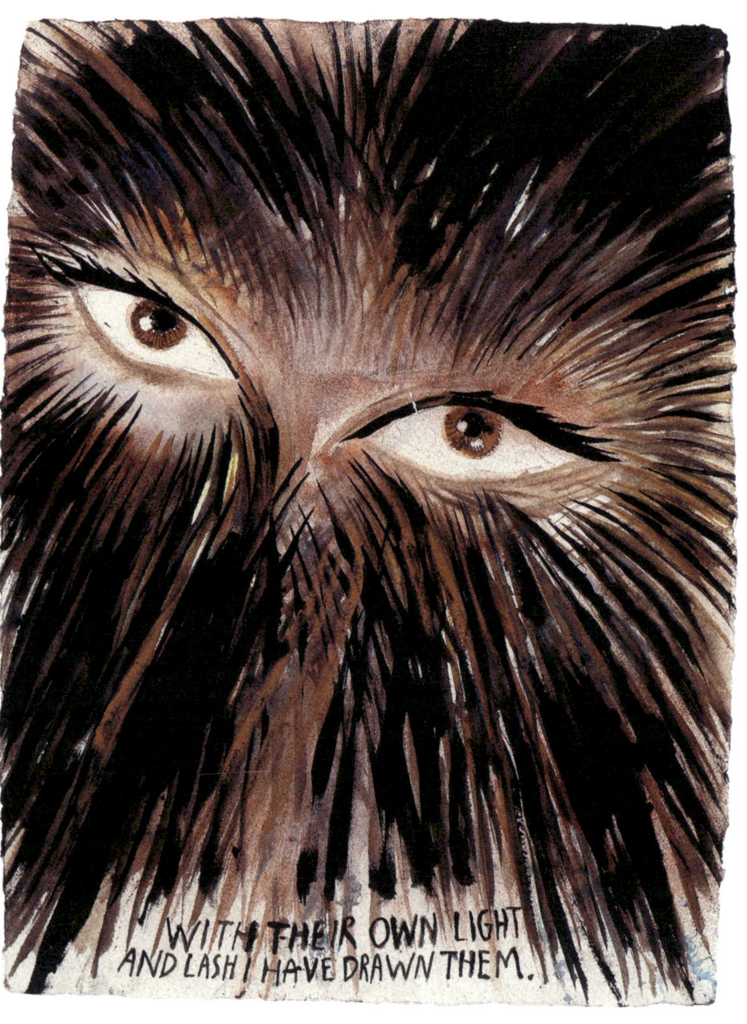WITH THEIR OWN LIGHT
AND LASH I HAVE DRAWN THEM.

Spiyt th'Words

Rereading Pettibon's Twitter

Andrew Durbin

The art of writing is the attempt to contain the teeming scrawl which everywhere threatens to gain the upper hand, in the interest of maintaining a halfway functional personality.

—W. G. Sebald

Twiytter suycks. Just giveme th'mfckn mic—

—Raymond Pettibon

I GATHERED THOUGHTS, MEANINGS
AND PRAYERS AT ONCE MORE BRIGHTLY
TRANSPARENT, YET MORE FORMIDABLE
THAN THE RUINS OF ILLUSTRIOUS
CITIES HAD EVER CALLED UP TO ME.

"titssand twttsss."

10:40 PM – 5 Feb 2011

**Gadhafi isn't target; civilians
are. Would set the wrong
precedent to hold heads of
state accountable.**

2:18 AM – 22 Mar 2011

6:00 PM – 21 Apr 2011

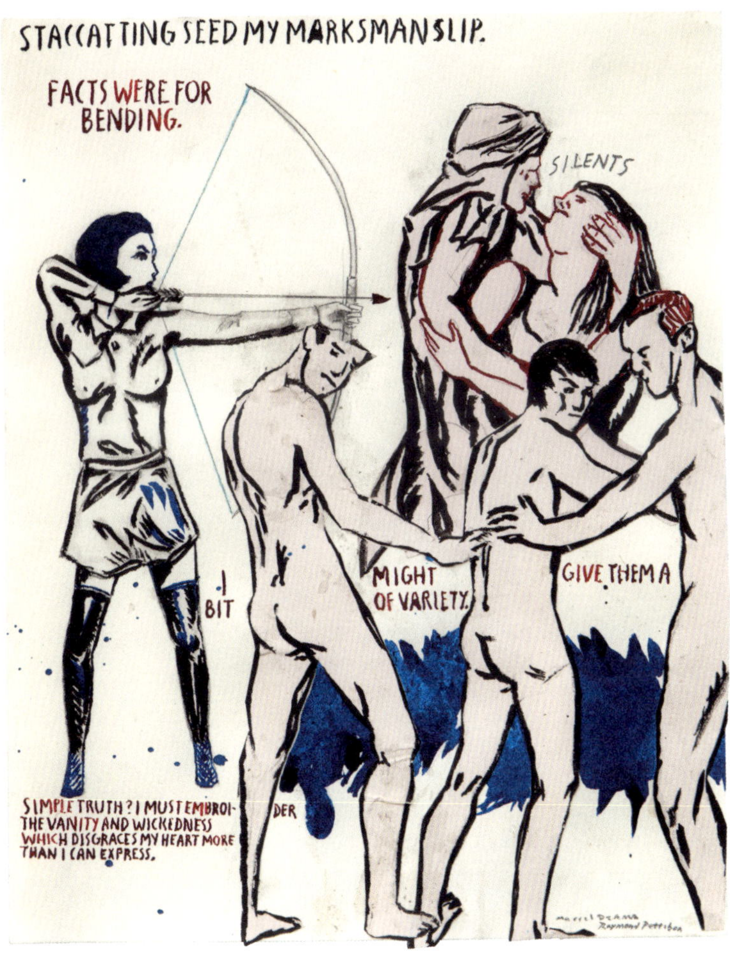

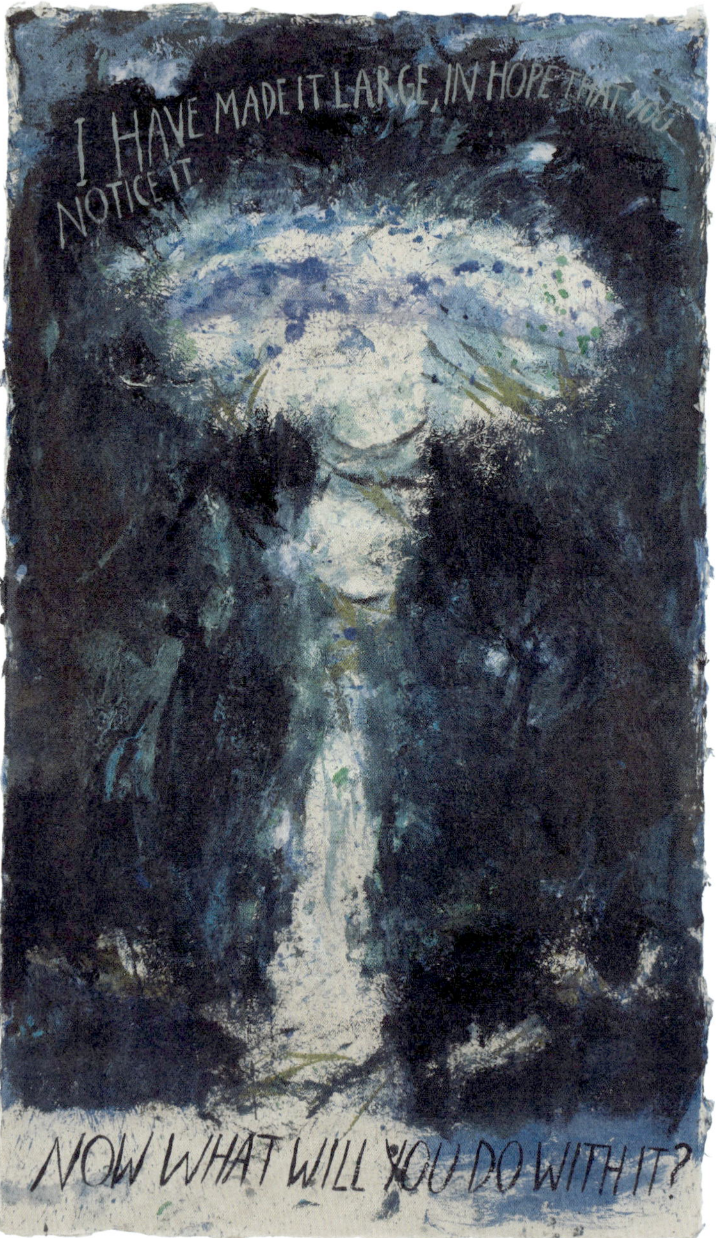
I HAVE MADE IT LARGE IN HOPE THAT YOU
NOTICE IT
NOW WHAT WILL YOU DO WITH IT?

**W Bush was/is a sociopath.
What's Obama's excuse?**

6:55 AM – 23 Apr 2011

U.S. Gov't: too big to fail.

9:26 PM – 9 Dec 2011

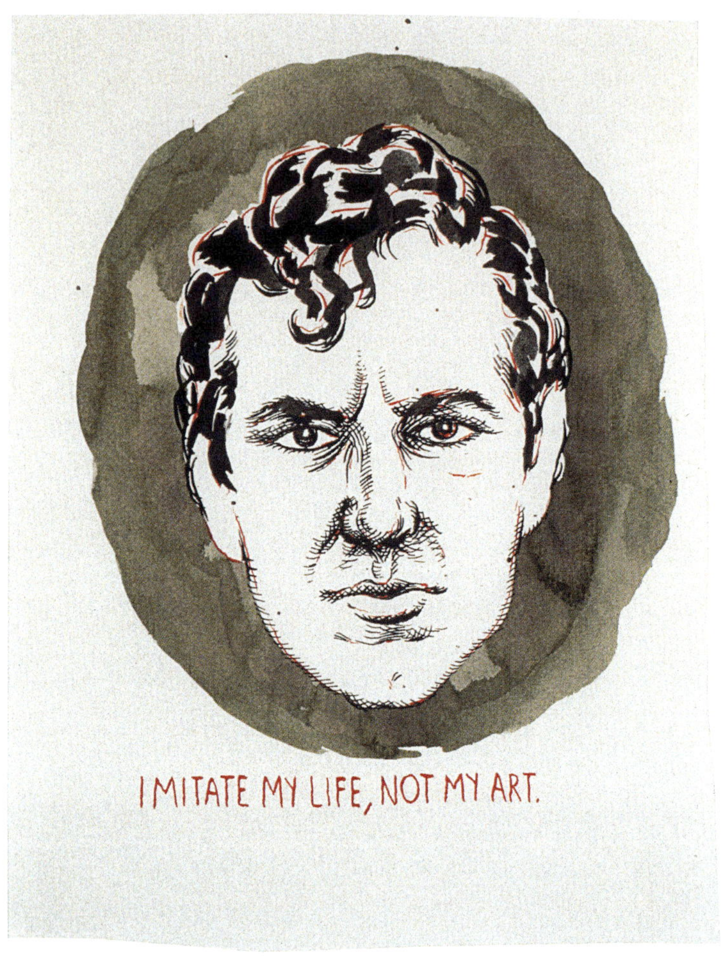

@yokoono You're planting
the seeds?Yr dropping
the bombs.CHitchens wld
be proud.Human lives
(Chicken Little dies too)
mean nothing 2 U?

11:03 AM – 10 Nov 2012

Art Worlders I know are agnst the violence in general.who speaks up but me?Silence=Death indeed.Lives and careers are at stake

5:01 PM – 17 Nov 2012

Tryccyck whuytup bytcch? Scycckk on this or stoyp yr Twittertwat:I like the btchs in the Hot Dog On A Stck:they are HOYYTT!

7:31 PM – 2 Dec 2012

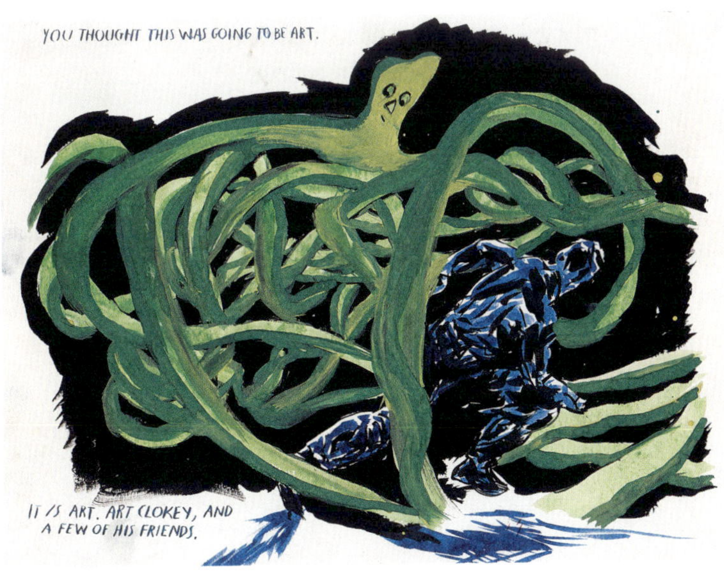

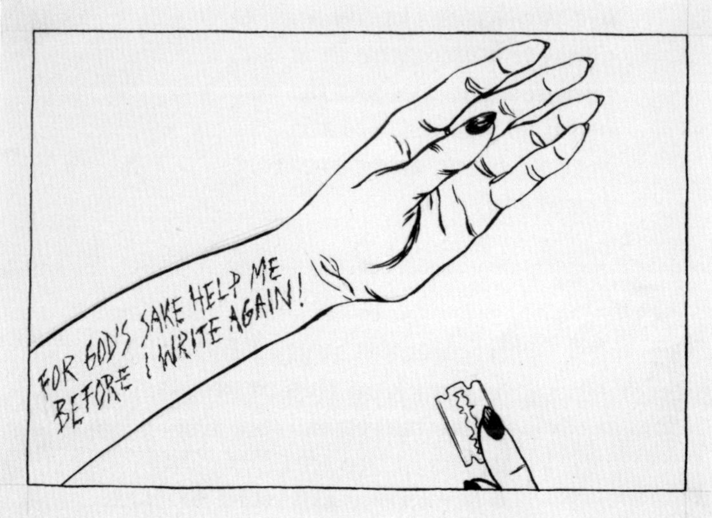

"I am a natural reader, and only a writer in the absence of natural writers. In a true time, I should never have written."—Sincerely, Ray

2:26 PM – 18 Jan 2013

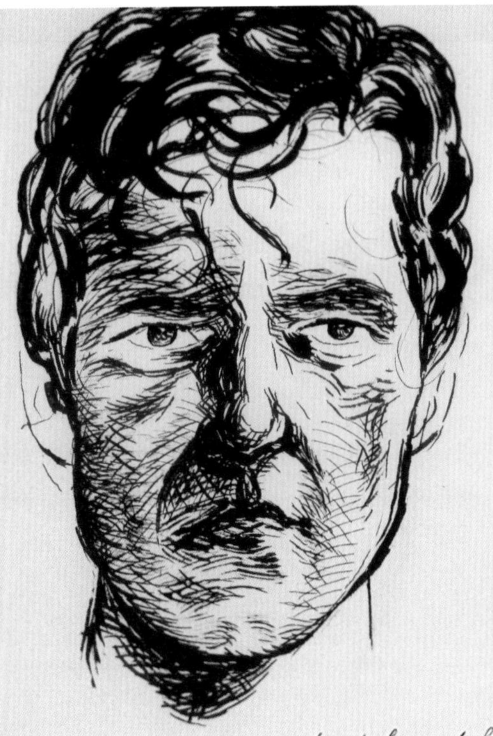

So occasional, so accidental, so full of the
echoes of voices that are not his -- not the artist's,
not the artist's muse, nor even the voice of the
man himself — that he is not to be trusted.

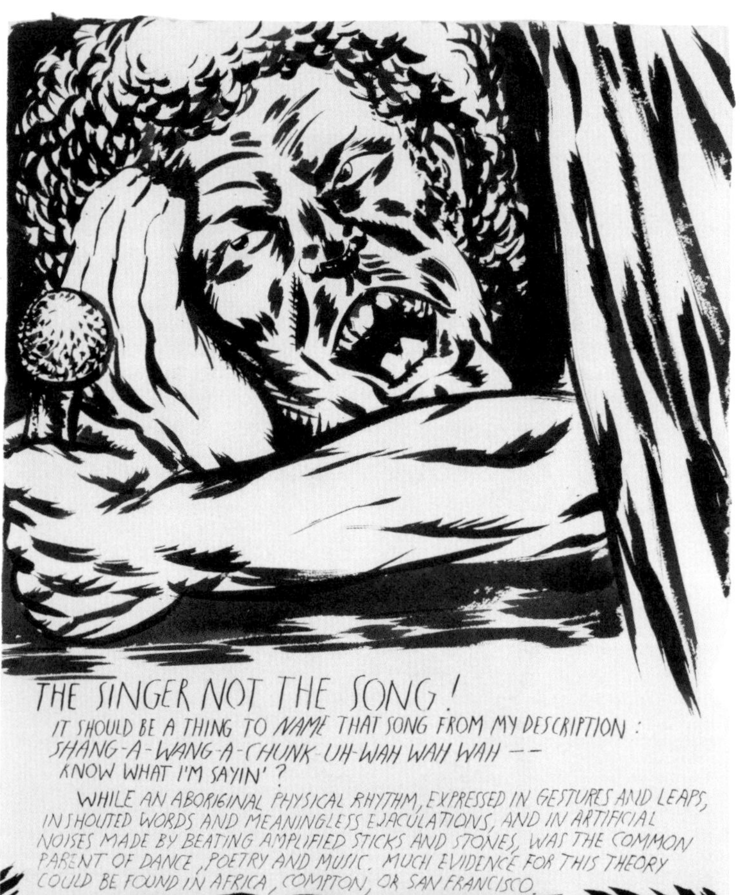

THE SINGER NOT THE SONG!
IT SHOULD BE A THING TO NAME THAT SONG FROM MY DESCRIPTION:
SHANG-A-WANG-A-CHUNK-UH-WAH WAH WAH —
KNOW WHAT I'M SAYIN'?
WHILE AN ABORIGINAL PHYSICAL RHYTHM, EXPRESSED IN GESTURES AND LEAPS,
IN SHOUTED WORDS AND MEANINGLESS EJACULATIONS, AND IN ARTIFICIAL
NOISES MADE BY BEATING AMPLIFIED STICKS AND STONES, WAS THE COMMON
PARENT OF DANCE, POETRY AND MUSIC. MUCH EVIDENCE FOR THIS THEORY
COULD BE FOUND IN AFRICA, COMPTON, OR SAN FRANCISCO.

Mayor Bloomberg n Norman Podhoretz Halloween all year round.Vampires who live forever on Palestinian boys' parts.Living abortions.

3:34 PM – 1 Nov 2013

Yr next Pres will be the cunt-munching wife o the syphlitic-herpes-Aids-ridden Bill:Hilary.Enjoy yr next 8 yrs following Sir Drone Obama

4:59 AM – 2 Nov 2013

PnkRckrsALWAYS claim they know me from pnk. Shoulda saved pennies n bought in fanboy chumps.U'd be $millionaires now. But tht wld be sellout.

6:11 PM – 25 Sep 2014

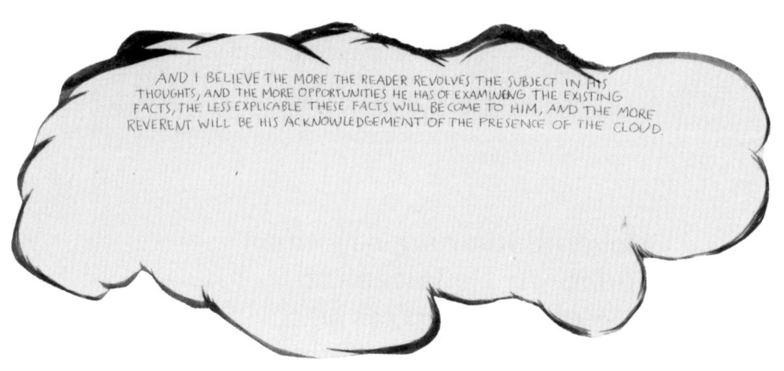

**Fck em all.Bomb,Bomb :
cauliflowered eared
mushroom cloud is enuff
shock n awe for any of us.
N xclamation point on
myTHE END!**

11:03 PM – 6 Oct 2014

Milhouse Nixon n BeBe?Well their longtime companionship ouytlasted RFK's w/Joe McC cuzz o hepatitusC.Obama's w/Bibi goin on 8yrs.Luyvfest.

4:36 AM – 10 Nov 2014

N' U 20 yr old 50 yr pnk rckrs:You ain't blank, so I'm leavin you.For pnckrckgardeneden. Sckmydck.

5:09 PM – 8 Sep 2015

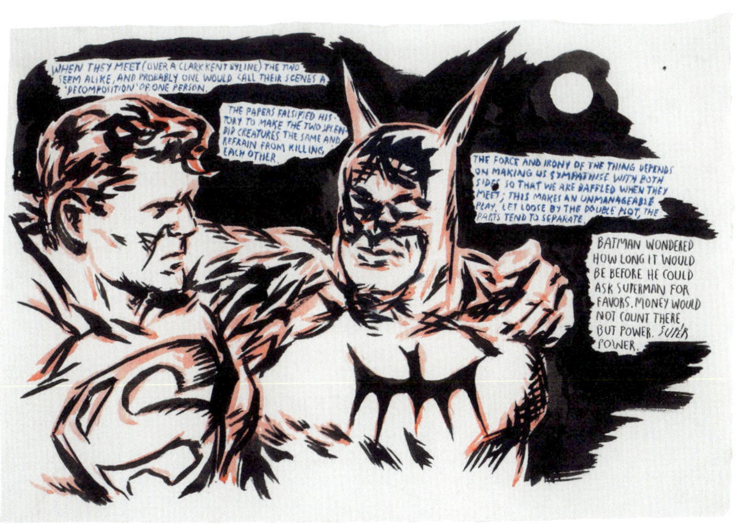

PnkRck a guvnr on Suspect
Device(U2?)LA Pnkrrs
aDORED,while their model
was Springstein.Sorry 4 nt
fanboy or pnk groupies ugly
as hellnoAIDS

9:37 PM – 4 Oct 2015

Whyno politic sabremetrics
4 politicians?Ruth hit 714 hr,
BoBonds WAR.Lincoln,
Wilson,FDR,JFK,LBJ,RMN,
WRostow,Kissinger.HnB,
OB:Killfild

1:03 AM – 19 Oct 2015

Who I'm 4. Think abouyt it
fooyls. 4 Self-Determination,
Peace, Diplomacy. Against
war, death, imperialism.
9:26 PM – 10 Mar 2016

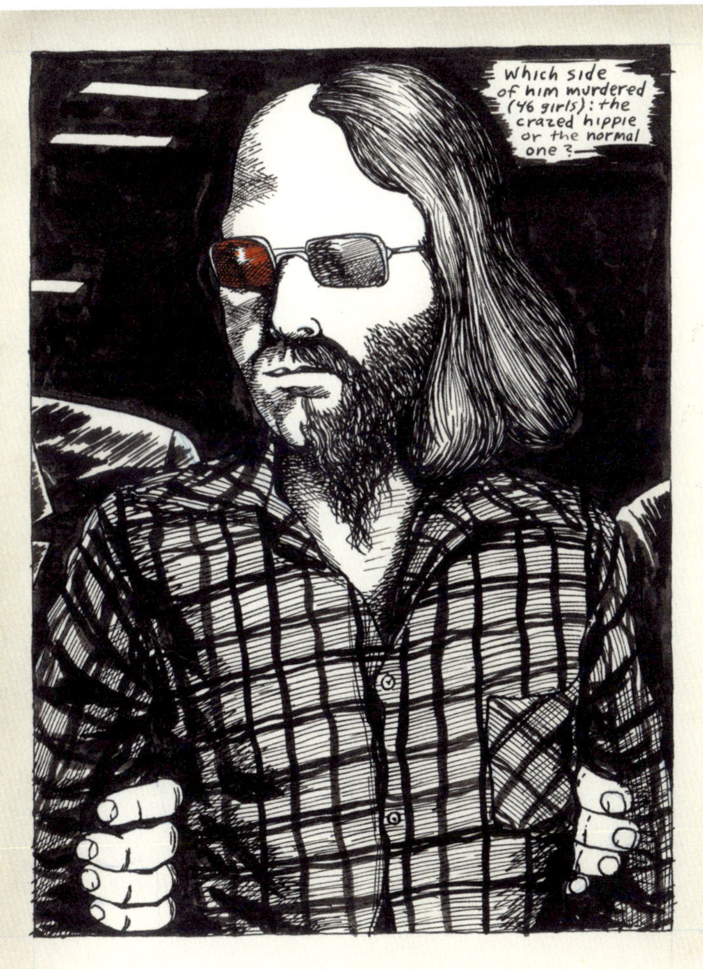

WHICH SIDE
of HIM murdered
(46 girls): the
crazed hippie
or the normal
one?

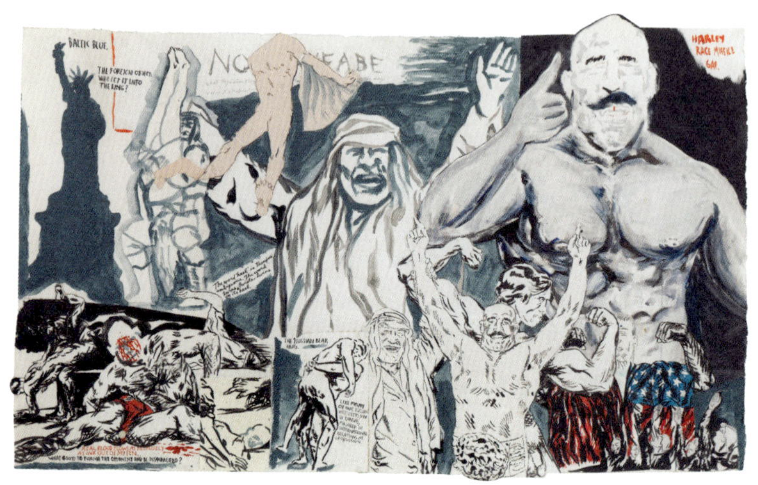

I thot I thaw a Tweeyty-Bird!---- You saw a Drone, fooyl.

4:13 AM – 26 Mar 2016

**Kanye:Gimme Zaha petro$'s
I'll build brand 4Dubai/
Saudi Royal Fams; will pimp
KKK to Arab world, come
2 yr Casbah, $weeyt 16
partie$$$**

6:29 PM – 2 Apr 2016

DOUBLE SELF-PORTRAIT.

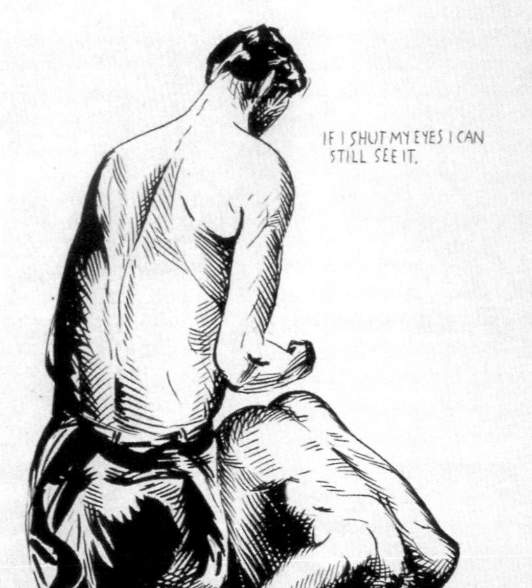
HE LOOKED LIKE A MAN WITH
A GOOD CAPACITY FOR HATRED.

IF I SHUT MY EYES I CAN
STILL SEE IT.

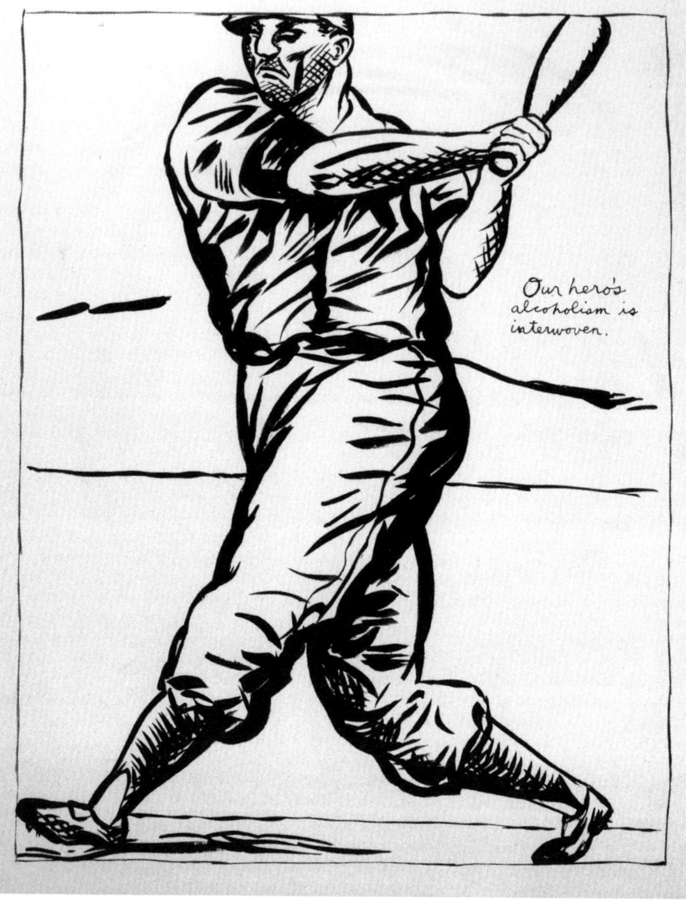

Our hero's
alcoholism is
interwoven.

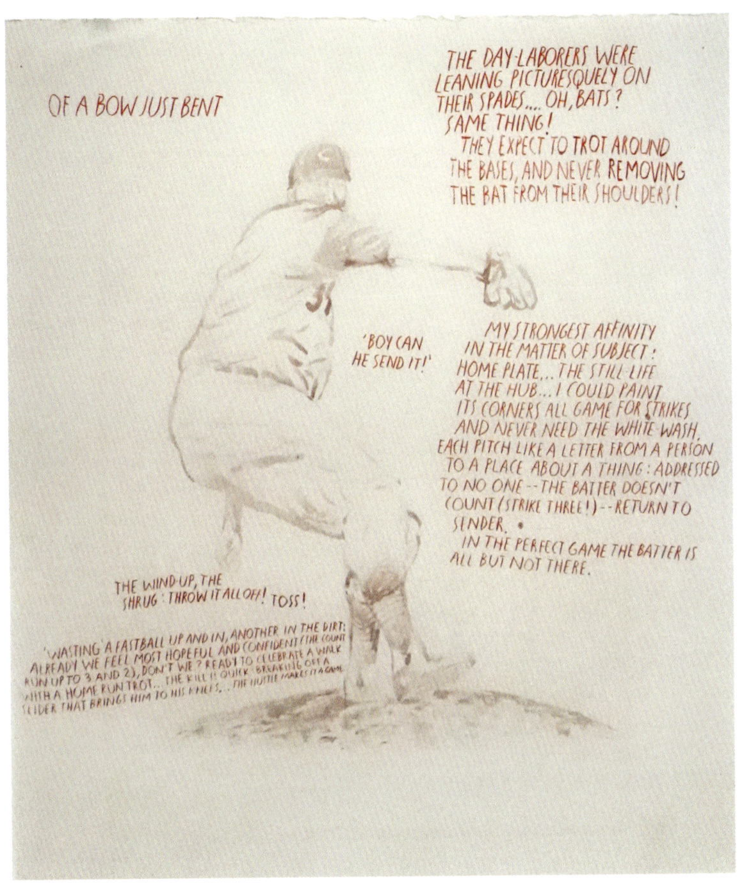

The vile,carcinogenic HilaryCANCER is in it 4 lonng term.The depleted uranium she dumps on innocents'll be ouytlasted by the Clinton Dynasty

3:52 PM – 4 May 2016

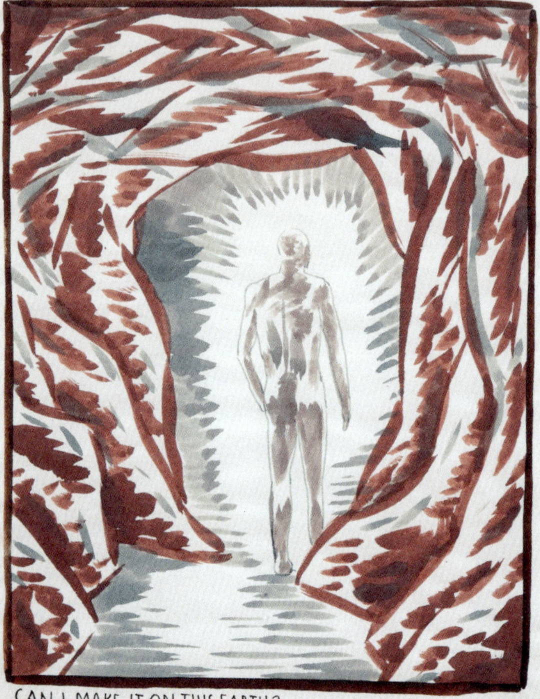

**Any1 seriously thnk
th'neolibcon Hilary was
4 protectng Balts,etc from
Russia? She wld have Israeli
sttlements built on WBank
o Ukraine.**

12:26 AM – 12 Jan 2017

**Real Political Thuygs dnt act
for the cameras. They ACT—
in silence and in stealth.**

2:45 PM – 21 Jan 2017

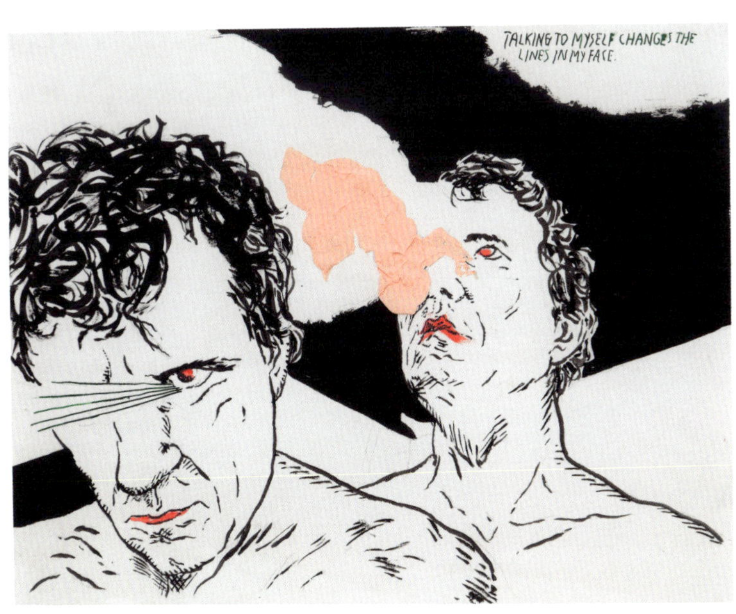

Legacy means nothing 2 me. When dead yr dead.The Retrospectives or BlackFAIL flyersLOL.But Greg Ginn's been main arbiter o my Wiki 4 years.

3:36 AM – 7 Feb 2017

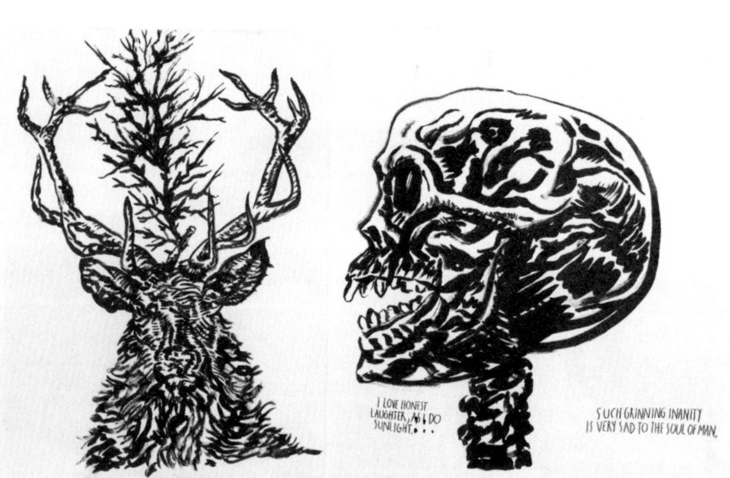

Admission: Orson Bean's emission at th'bathhouse Cleveland OH b4 Tattletales Gameshow gave me th'edge won me $2500; is tht cheating?

10:47 PM – 7 Feb 2017

Truymp's upfront racism is sickening. So do something abouyt iyt.But Clinton built n filld the PrisonIndustrial Projects.nRickRossObama C.O.

7:39 PM – 12 Mar 2017

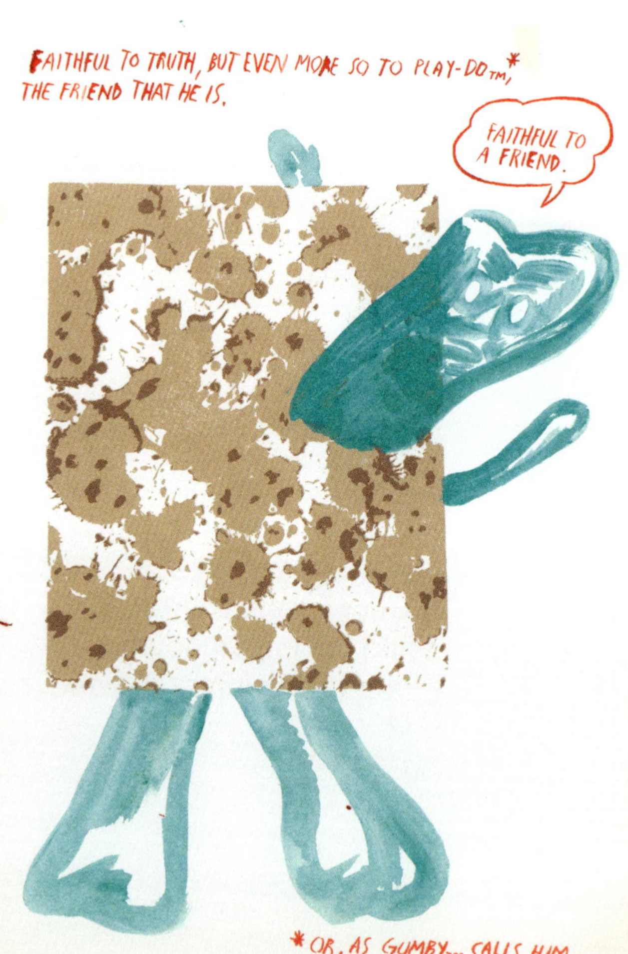

FAITHFUL TO TRUTH, BUT EVEN MORE SO TO PLAY-DO™,*
THE FRIEND THAT HE IS.

* OR, AS GUMBY™ CALLS HIM,
PLATO.

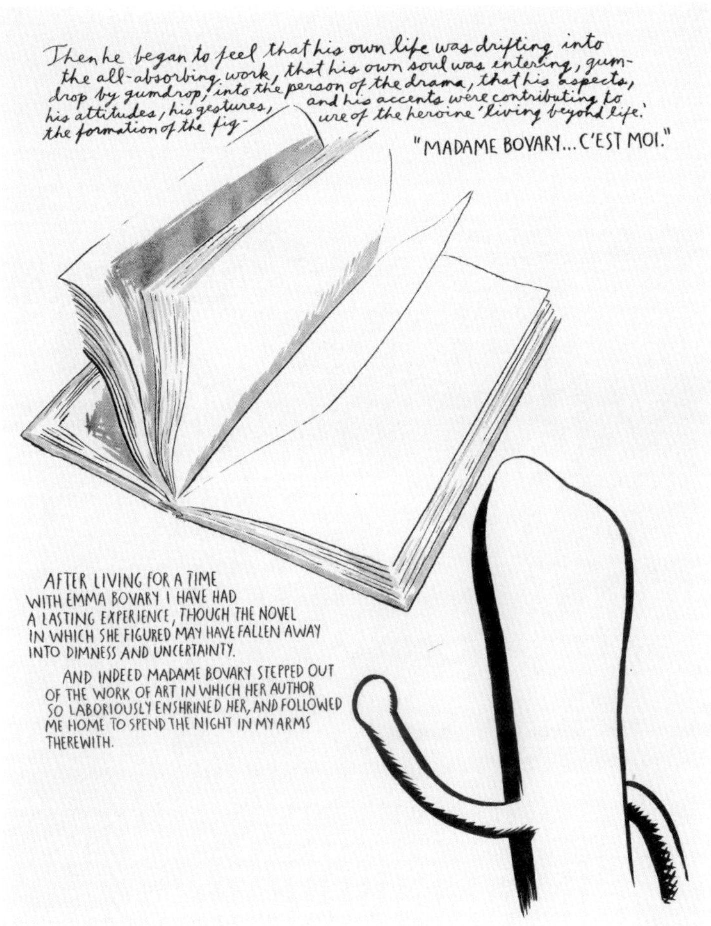

**at 579 BroadwayStudio2C.
Homies DeLonte West n
Dauntayy Jones came thru.
No Kardahians/Wintours.**

5:21 PM – 3 May 2017

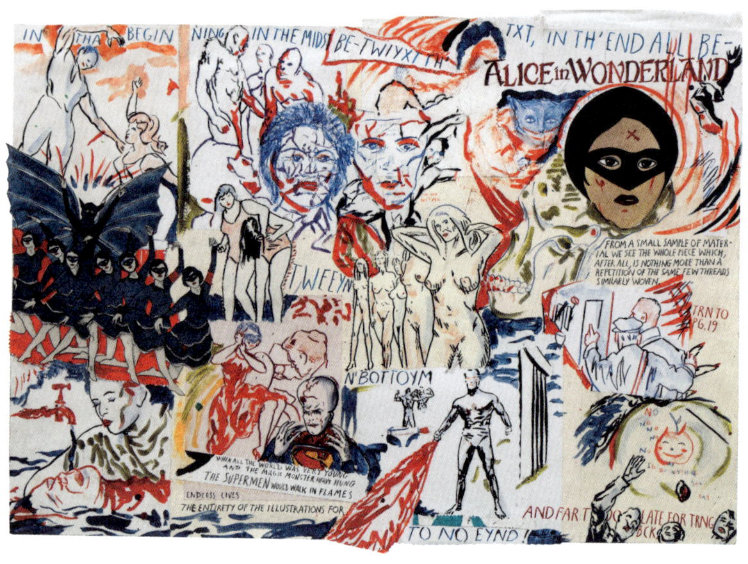

I've goyt a story 2 tell...
leyt iyt driyp,driyp ouyt
my dck on twiyt.Patience?
call CPS. Readng Proust
again, Vo.3.Bouyt time.
My self-help bk

11:39 AM – 3 Jun 2017

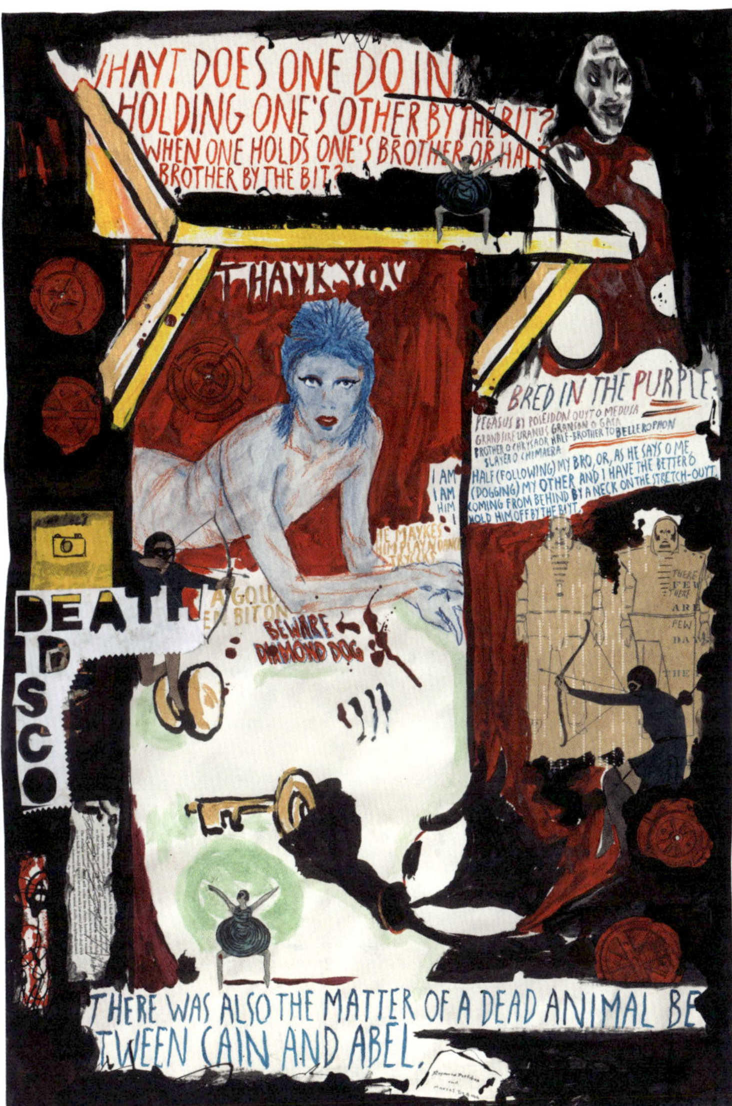

WHAYT DOES ONE DO IN HOLDING ONE'S OTHER BY THE BIT?
WHEN ONE HOLDS ONE'S BROTHER OR HALF
BROTHER BY THE BIT?
THANK YOU
BRED IN THE PURPLE:
PEGASUS BY POSEIDON OUYT O MEDUSA
GRAND SIRE URANUS GRANDAM O GAIA
BROTHER O CHRYSAOR HALF-BROTHER TO BELLEROPHON
SLAYER O CHIMAERA
HALF (FOLLOWING) MY BRO, OR, AS HE SAYS O ME
(DOGGING) MY OTHER AND I HAVE THE BETTER O
KOMING FROM BEHIND BY A NECK ON THE STRETCH-OUYT
HOLD HIM OFF BY THE BAYT
I AM
I AM
HIM
HE MAYKES
HIM PLAY N DANCE
TRYCKES
A GOLD
BIT ON
BEWARE
DIAMOND DOG
DEATH
DISCO
THERE
FEW
THERE
ARE
FEW
DAY
THE
THERE WAS ALSO THE MATTER OF A DEAD ANIMAL BE
TWEEN CAIN AND ABEL.

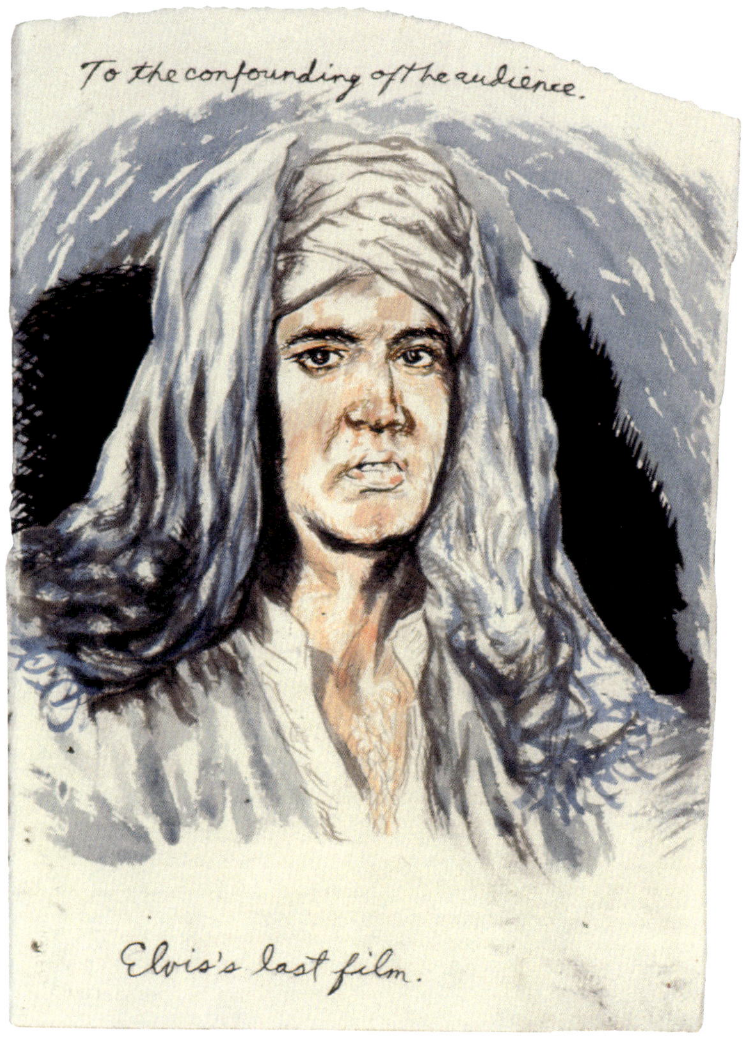

To the confounding of the audience.

Elvis's last film.

1

On February 5, 2011, the artist Raymond Pettibon tweeted for the first time at 10:40 p.m.: **"titssand twttsss."**

2

One possible translation: "tits and twats," though the latter word might be read, in the original, as a Pettibon-variant spelling of "tweets" or "twits" ("a silly or foolish person"), or even transliterated birdsong, the *tweet tweet tweet* of the blue chickadee that serves as the platform's avian symbol. In 2011, Twitter was still a mostly text-based social media platform, without the heavy emphasis on images that now marks the feed; pics of tits and twats were once much harder to find. A tit is a noisy bird, of course, found all over the world, *twttsss*.

Pettibon's profile image is a detail from a drawing of his, *No Title (With their own . . .)*, 2007. It shows a werewolf's face with two large, yearning eyes set deep in a hairy mask, like that of a doe-eyed Chewbacca you might find on the cover of the *Weekly World News*: "Beast Lets Loose on Local Foes." Wiry hair shoots from the center of the animal's noseless face. Her long lashes, her black eyeliner, suggest that perhaps she's a werewoman, one who succeeds in a two-hundred-year line of eminent shebeasts, beginning with Catherine Crowe's 1846 "A Story of a Weir-Wolf," the first known English-language tale of woman-to-wolf transformation.

In Pettibon's drawing, she's sympathetic, even somewhat flirty (her eyes twinkle with cryptic desire). Since he first signed on, the wolf has faithfully served as Pettibon's digital head. I take her for him.

She might step out of the closet, into your bedroom in the middle of the night, and apologize for the accident of her unexpected presence. What brought her around? Eying your untidy room, she growls, "Whayt?"

3

In the full drawing, Pettibon wrote under his werewolf:

WITH THEIR OWN LIGHT
AND LASH I HAVE DRAWN THEM.

Is the phrase spoken by her or is it stray commentary that found its way into the artist's head after he'd finished the work, a caption meant to deepen the drawing's tiny enigma rather than illustrate the figure's point of view, something she might be telling us?

Whom has she drawn to her? Or is she among "them"?

[*A whip cracks.*] WEIR-WOLF, or WEIRA [*pronounced* "VERA"]: "Wake!"

Her face is his as much as hers. A beast apart, but one who shares (or at least sympathizes with) his predilections, his politics, his friends, and his enemies.

[*A whip cracks twice.*] WEIRA: "Not gonna say it again."

In the artist's rangy body of work, the relationship between a picture and language is complex, irregular, and sometimes obscure. Often the text—handwritten below, above, or across the page—appears to have been spoken by a character, as in a comic; in other drawings, sentences read like incantatory koans, recorded by their author as a kind of back-of-the-head dream speech, id's spew. On Twitter, Pettibon cribs his art's ensemble approach, though he reduces the number of characters, or speakers, to one: @raymondpettibon—a flippant, funny, and gabby mouthpiece for strange voices (his or not, we're left to wonder). It comes close to what I imagine the artist-not-making-art might be thinking about, too: sports, music, politics, and so on. Sort of. It bears a strong resemblance to his writing on the drawings, and like that writing, the words never quite belong to him, but rather to the litany of voices he calls forth to speak in his place. It's not not-art, is the thing.

WEIRA: "Get . . . up . . ."

I'm up. Pettibon has about 25,700 followers, as of this writing. He in turn follows 15,100 accounts.

4

I joined Twitter in 2011, in the early days of the Arab Spring, when the sleepy platform was transformed, seemingly overnight, into a source of rapid, rambling, and confused accounts of the revolts and revolutions in Egypt, Libya, Syria, and Tunisia, told through the tweets of organizers and protesters on the so-called Arab Street. All of this was captured in 140-character newsflashes that reported where the crowds had gathered and which cities had taken up arms against their doomed national governments.

This was a marked difference from other social media platforms. How else could we watch a revolution in *real time*, and in Syria? Twitter provided a fast-moving, multi-perspective view (told mostly by strangers) of a conflict that seemed then to possess an urgent and impressive democratic spirit. There was a certain heady, misplaced utopianism to this belief, too, especially in the US, where we were all basically screwed in our colonial cluelessness. Still, that utopianism didn't appear far from the actual revolutionary politics germinating in the occupation of Cairo's Tahrir Square.

I didn't know what would come of what we watched.

5

The news, particularly long-form Western journalism, which was at once dismissive and overly optimistic of the protests, became an irrelevant appendix to Twitter, a wordy catalog of newspaper observers who had no real way of knowing what was happening among the—and this is a mouthful—Arab *aganaktismenoi* (the Greek word for "the movement of the squares" that was used to describe the near simultaneous anti-austerity, anti-European Union protests in Athens at the time).

Directed largely at a corrupt political class and the austerity measures enforced by American and European governments, global discontent spanned three continents, extending from Damascus to Tripoli to New York, where the Occupy movement seized Zuccotti Park in the fall of that year (organized, in part, on Twitter) and managed to cling to its small square of Manhattan until winter. Then to the West Coast, where the University of California, Berkeley campus and the Port of Oakland became the staging grounds for numerous demonstrations, riots, and occupations.

There was a mood—neither hopeful nor pessimistic but, in almost every instance, something else, a tingling sense of charged release, born of a long period of repressed rage—that people were fighting back, or at least taking up a collective cause, and they weren't necessarily losing. It was a foggy year, with so many actions it is difficult to recall their exact order: when did Tripoli fall, and did it? I stuffed my face with pizza in a line of poets near Ground Zero, the sound of the People's Mic echoing in the rain. Friends recited their poems against the cops. The cops stood by, their big guns in hand. We were pitiful but I loved the smallness of our lot.

There was Gezi Park in Turkey, which was in 2013, though I remember it as part of this continuum of protests and, in my mind, it belongs with us in 2011.

Syriza in Greece, though that was in 2012.

Where, and when, was Oakland?

Things were in a jumble and, in my memory, the events of and around this time lie in disarray.

That year's insurrections were each different in their specified (or, in some cases, strategically unspecified) demands. While the Arab popular uprisings varied substantially from the Greek and American riots and occupations, all had resulted from a resentment against an upbraiding economic system, administered globally by authoritarian governments conjoined in their financial aims with multinational business, that had, for decades, ensured that poor people stayed in their place while autocrats, oligarchs, and executives made a boozy run for most of the world's resources, and virtually all of the world's wealth.

In this disorienting fog, many of us signed up for Twitter to see what and where the grand and expanding Event was happening, and for the first time in our lives (for the first time in my life) we could know exactly what people were doing elsewhere, either in riot or protest, and in *real time*. We were seeking a form of clarity, an eye on things, the things themselves: an order, if not *the* order.

6

And in that watershed year, Pettibon was there . . . sort of.

Gadhafi isn't target; civilians are. Would set the wrong precedent to hold heads of state accountable.

2:18 AM – 22 Mar 2011

W Bush was/is a sociopath. What's Obama's excuse?

6:55 AM – 23 Apr 2011

U.S. Gov't: too big to fail.

9:26 PM – 9 Dec 2011

7

Sort of . . . not, too. Pettibon's writing on the platform is a scramble of quotations, in-jokes, incendiary critique, obvious or vague gibes at enemies or allies, sometimes in overt, sharp-tongued political rejoinders:

Mayor Bloomberg n Norman Podhoretz Halloween all year round.Vampires who live forever on Palestinian boys' parts. Living abortions.

3:34 PM – 1 Nov 2013

The tweets occasionally appear in his more perplexing, Y-ridden vernacular:

Tryccyck whuytup bytcch? Scycckk on this or stoyp yr Twittertwat:I like the btchs in the Hot Dog On A Stck:they are HOYYTT!

7:31 PM – 2 Dec 2012

Unlike those who use Twitter to establish their *singular* voice as part of an event or series of events, as part of a place or a riot or an occupation or a restaurant or a movie or a soon-to-be viral incident involving a celebrity, Pettibon seldom has any interest in contextualizing himself in *real time*, in the *real time* of present things—or tweets. (Which isn't to say he's not around, only that he's just that: *around*.) Instead, he appears mixed up in his own imbroglios, which are sometimes ours, but almost always his.

His tweets look askance at the contemporary moment and don't obey the usual rules of Twitter (pithy, concise humor; fact-based assistance or information; or even the dreaded thread, wherein a user strings together a numbered argument or story—popular after the election of the forty-fifth president, and an utterly dismal reading experience for those who follow the form). Instead, Pettibon is closer to what's called "weird Twitter," the popular segment of the platform composed of users who tweet, with off-kilter humor, non-sequiturs or near gibberish, oftentimes misspelled (@dril) or in a deliberate imitation of Twitter's many fritzing bots (@Horse_ebooks). Pettibon's own account isn't a coherent text, at least not in any traditional sense: a contained or semi-contained work, start to finish linked by a recognizable arc or argument. It doesn't have the ambition to achieve coherence, to be read from beginning to end (few do, besides those bots that tweet out full texts like *Moby-Dick* or the complete works of Shakespeare). Instead, he's comprehensive in his rage and melancholy and disappointment and praise, his feelings of defeat and of pyrrhic victory, his akimbo politics. Pettibon's feed obtains the novelistic or literary strain found in his drawings, which likewise go on and on, in deference to a world without narrative, comprised solely of fragments, shored against . . . There are recurring characters: mostly actual people, like Hillary Clinton, Donald Trump (spelled Truymp), Pettibon's brother, his son, Yoko Ono, Norman Podhoretz. He has tweeted or retweeted over 40,000 times, which makes his overall feed difficult to review, given the platform's relatively cumbersome advanced search feature. His Twitter is both separate from his art and a wily, perturbed, and prosaic extension of it—a beast apart.

WEIRA [*smirking*]: "Or within."

The sprawling nature of the platform is probably part of its appeal to Pettibon (on it, he himself sprawls), the fact that it doesn't tell a straightforward story—as, say, a blog would.

The transmissions from his world are peculiar and reflect his elliptical alliances with, and animosities toward, politicos, subgroups, dead and living artists, each of which he upholds or forgets on a whim, so to write about the artist's feed requires a certain amount of speculation, since a great deal of what he says—

**Puyt hoop bck uyp on
th'hardscrabknockfloor at 579
BroadwayStudio2C. Homies DeLonte
West n Dauntayy Jones came thru.
No Kardahians/Wintours.**

5:21 PM – 3 May 2017

—is oblique, even to those familiar with his lexical and analytic strategies (that proliferating Y), and occurs within a somewhat willfully unknowable mind. Pettibon doesn't seem to want to be fully understood—or, rather, being understood is beside the point:

**Trck: Ilose my MFKN patience I'm through
typing dint go to tyoping scool btch im
for real lisssten**

6:00 PM – 21 Apr 2011

**I've goyt a story 2 tell…leyt iyt driyp,driyp
ouyt my dck on twiyt.Patience?call CPS.
Readng Proust again, Vo.3.Bouyt time.
My self-help bk**

11:39 AM – 3 Jun 2017

In Proust's *Guermantes Way*, the third volume of *In Search of Lost Time*, the narrator navigates a gossipy, prewar Paris, where the wealthy host dinner parties as Europe gears up to self-incinerate. Pettibon maps a similarly dire territory of rich and depraved personalities caught up in Dantesque tableaux, but his America isn't quite the twilight Paris of *À la recherche*, with its delicate worship of the social codes of the nineteenth century. Proust's arriviste protagonist envies the rich men and women around him, adores and even joins them regardless of whatever doubt he harbors about their doomed city; Pettibon is utterly disturbed by our world's mincing elite, in whose terrible hands all our fates rest.

8

Pettibon's approach to Twitter—often bombastic, even seditious—has made for many bizarre moments in Twitter's pitched traffic. Yoko Ono once served, over the course of many tweets, as a broadly drawn villain opposed to world peace. For a time, he couldn't drop the feud, and his accusations against her became increasingly grand: she was guilty of war crimes, or at least covered for war criminals, like General David Petraeus, who oversaw US military operations in the Middle East and Central Asia. She was cozy with the conservative writer Christopher Hitchens. She had pulled the trigger, dropped the bomb, gassed the innocent. It largely made no sense. When Ono tweeted:

#100Acorns – 100 days of instructions & artworks – Follow on #Instagram at instagram.com/100acorns

8:44 AM – 10 Nov 2012

Pettibon responded:

@yokoono You're planting the seeds?Yr dropping the bombs.CHitchens wld be proud.Human lives(Chicken Little dies too) mean nothing 2 U?

11:03 AM – 10 Nov 2012

Who's this?

Since his earliest work, Pettibon has made use of the mean and reproachful voices of the extreme right, the chatter of murderers and cultish strongmen, and the rumor-mongering of the nefarious personalities who skulk at the outer edges of traditional public discourse. They are all, in their own way, hangovers of the doomed pleasures and terminal utopias of the 1960s, and Pettibon deploys them to disrupt received narratives of power, fame, and history, particularly when the target is a president or an actual war criminal, like Henry Kissinger, or even a celebrated figure in pop culture, like Mickey Mouse, who has appeared in the artist's work as a demented pied piper ("All my groupies are 9, 10 years old at the most," one drawing reads).

In "After Laughter," Benjamin H. D. Buchloh notes that Pettibon deliberately "speaks in the language of the enemy" rather than cough up the decorous language of public life, upheld by politicians, newspapers, and television reporters so as to remove "any 'outside' that would allow the speaker and the listener the privilege of distantiating derision." Pettibon scours the riven, frustrated speech—the "tropes of sleaze," Buchloh writes—of individuals prone to violence and excess and fear and base need in what the critic calls the artist's "dark caricature, the caricature after laughter." This darkly comic mode suspends laughter "in response to the violence of the circumstances under which the joke is produced," resulting in a condition of "totalized implication." We each have our seats saved in the audience.

Twitter, it seems, is no different. Or its difference is medium-specific: without the blank piece of paper to bring those voices out in the hand-drawn faces of presidents and kooks, Pettibon makes himself—his feed—their face.

"Paint the all unutterable," one work from 1991 reads, in what might be read as a condensed thesis for Pettibon's interest in the verboten language of extremism—the "all unutterable"—that finds its way into many of his drawings, where figures describe ugly feelings, crave terrible things, and give in to their worst fears. "All I care about is nukes," one 1982 drawing of a meditating man reads. From a 1984 work: "I've prayed for nuclear war every day since 1945." A 2007 drawing depicting Klansmen around a burning cross: "We have applied it ourselves to the current problems of American society. We have endeavored to light up with it the southern sky." One woman looks at the moon in a 1986 ink and gouache on paper: "A certain Donald Trump. The first real gentleman I'd met in years." Pettibon has long channeled the seething voices that gurgle below the surface of American life, and he has made use of their confounding language to create equally confounding scenes of anger, fear, resentment, and hate: the American mode.

On Twitter, he applies this polyvocal approach to authorship to a point of almost deranged absurdity, making himself an ongoing sketch wherein vile speech cycles through his feed as he targets the usual suspects of the far right's anger, like Hillary Clinton and other liberal politicians. Much of it is paltry compared to what one finds on actual right-wing message boards, but nonetheless awful. With Ono, as with many celebrities who have been the target of Pettibon's ire over the years, it appears, on the surface, blistering and fucked up, but obviously so (hatred of Ono has long been the calling card of white male resentment toward women—and Asian—artists)—and I don't believe we can interpret his feed as if it's strictly the artist voicing his opinion, even if it is strictly @raymondpettibon typing.

Truymp writes my twiyts.

10:59 PM – 20 June 2017

He has tweeted his opposition to politicians of every party, though few have received as much scorn as Clinton, who once served as his most serious foe in many hundreds of tweets, from her time as Secretary of State to her failed second bid for the presidency. In criticizing Clinton, Pettibon deploys a hectic, demented array of voices, some recognizably his own (Pettibon undoubtedly dislikes and distrusts her)

and some far angrier, far more baroque in their churlish language—
usually centered on Clinton's body—to condemn the state-sanctioned
violence she is responsible for:

**Yr next Pres will be the cunt-munching
wife o the syphlitic-herpes-Aids-ridden
Bill:Hilary.Enjoy yr next 8 yrs following
Sir Drone Obama**

4:59 AM – 2 Nov 2013

**The vile,carcinogenic HilaryCANCER is in
it 4 lonng term.The depleted uranium she
dumps on innocents'll be ouytlasted by the
Clinton Dynasty**

3:52 PM – 4 May 2016

The words are difficult to read, but their difficulty, their explicit
ugliness, as with the difficulty and ugliness of his drawings, seems to
be their point. A bigoted tweet does not mean Pettibon has adopted
that position; rather, he turns the common Twitter bio line—"a retweet
doesn't equal an endorsement"—upside down by applying to the platform the same logic that drives his polyvocal drawings: This writing
does not equal me. But perhaps it equals *you,* even *us.*

9

Then there's his face.

WEIRA: "*His.* At last."

1990: the artist's *My Heart Tells Me (Self-Portrait).* A strikingly emotional work, Pettibon appears to us in his mid-forties, his handsome face
not yet wrinkled with age. Crow's-feet meet the corners of his eyes—the

44

most arresting feature of the drawing. A single tear slides down his left cheek. Pettibon's shirt collar is undone and falls loosely around his neck. He is at once rugged and boyish, as if the drawing were based on a publicity headshot for an accomplished actor of minor Westerns. The caption reads:

MY HEART TELLS ME THAT YOU WILL NOT LISTEN TO MY WORDS AND THIS IS THE CAUSE OF MY TEARS AND CRIES.

Cross-reference the drawing with 1996's *No Title (Imitate my life . . .)*, another self-portrait. Pettibon's silvery head floats like an Angeleno Wizard of Oz in a blotchy, brown cloud on yellow paper. Six years on, his face has hardened—his eyes, lips, nose are more defined in thatched penmanship—and he commands:

IMITATE MY LIFE, NOT MY ART

In several of the self-portraits, Pettibon roots his art in a conflicting binary, where two objects or ideas—what is said, what is heard; life, art—are placed at odds and from which he contrives an image animated by, though not always simply illustrative of, the irreconcilability of the dialectic he presents to the viewer. Like the humbug Wizard, he is two at once: an illusion and a man, an illustration and an artist. In his collected works, *Homo Americanus*, he maintains that his self-portraiture is "more than about making a drawing of myself." They are "too personal," but also "not personal": "they're about self-portraiture, rather than being self-portraits . . . there's the self in art and writing, to some degree. And to be entirely selfless is an attempt that I think fails. At its most elemental you got the Henry James story with the 'I' as the dick or the wiener."

Driven by contradictory forces from within and without, Pettibon's Ray struggles to reconcile the conceptual and emotional poles he finds himself pulled between, and the attendant mental agony plays out on the page and across his face: What am I to do? he always seems to ask, his expression soured with doubt. Another from 1990: *No Title (Double self-portrait . . .)*, a curious, dark drawing of the artist seemingly spanking or beating a humbled iteration of himself. The aggressor-Pettibon stands over the submissive-Pettibon with his back to the viewer, his shirt wrapped around his waist. This daddy—aren't all men of power in Pettibon's pantheon, whether it's himself or Charles Manson or the president, daddies of some kind or another, cock out and ready to condemn the world because of a bruised ego, a troubled past, a lost love—appears with his fist lowered over the rear of the sub, whose ass is raised up to receive a spanking. The caption, hovering above the Pettibon-dom, reads:

HE LOOKED LIKE A MAN WITH A GOOD CAPACITY FOR HATRED.

And to the right of his unseen face:

IF I SHUT MY EYES I CAN STILL SEE IT.

In much of Pettibon's work, the self is inseparable from its double, its inverse, or its negation. Our troubling ideas, our self-devouring wants, animate our outward lives and strive, rowdy beasts that they are, to break out, into the world, to highjack us, to make us do our worst. Pettibon consistently identifies an almost unbearable conflict at the heart of private and public American life, where two aspects of the world (and the self) must make peace with one another but can't.

WEIRA: "Me n 'im. Split—twiyt, seylf."

Pettibon often pictures himself in a brawl with differing aspects of his own personality, where one side of his thinking never overcomes the other, but rather attempts to coexist in a dueling, catastrophic perpetuity. Artist and writer, dom and sub, drawing and Twitter. It is this peculiar play between doubles that gives way to the intense self-*doubt*, produced by an overwhelming recognition of one's responsibilities to both the present and history, that is, in all its psychic forms, a singularly generative point of departure for him. In *No Title (Self-portrait. Richer . . .)*, 2001, Pettibon turns his back to us:

SELF-PORTRAIT.

RICHER BY ALL THE TOIL AND SUFFERING OF THE GENERATIONS THAT HAVE PRECEDED, AND BY THE FURTHER UNFOLDING OF THE ETERNAL PURPOSES.

HARD-BOUND.

A LOT IS RIDING ON THAT BACK.

In doubting the efficacy of language, art, communication, the assumptions of the winners and the losers, present things and time immemorial's backlog of junk, Pettibon repeatedly seeks out answers for himself and his past (his life and his art), whoever and whatever that may be at the time, only to find there are no good answers. Or, at least, no reasonable ones. And so, he must move on to the next drawing, scene, subject, supplication.

The Pettibon of the self-portraits is a Janus-faced cipher whose cryptic meaning always seems to pass over the horizon as soon as one begins to approach it. In a 1998 artist's book, *Self-Portraits My Ass*, Pettibon folds that horizon into the spine of a book, splitting himself across pages into a Rorschach-blot self, where one image mirrors another. The book's format doesn't quite hold throughout, as in one spread where the recto shows the artist in drag and the verso in a close-up of his worried brow.

He captions a 2014 self-portrait:

TALKING TO MYSELF CHANGES THE LINES IN MY FACE.

And in an older work, *No Title (So occasional, so . . .)*, 1992, he writes in slinking cursive what might be read as an artist's statement regarding both the drawings and the Twitter:

So occasional, so accidental, so full of the echoes of voices that are not his—not the artist's, not the artist's muse, not even the voice of the man himself—that he is not to be trusted.

The voices squawk in rage, simper with desire, whisper rumor with unearned confidence. They rattle off truth, confirm hearsay. They offer their provisional feelings only to fall back into the confusion of overheard chatter.

10

January 2016: *Marcel Dzama and Raymond Pettibon: Forgetting the Hand*, an exhibition at David Zwirner, New York, for which I contributed a poem to a zine published on the occasion of the show. At the opening, Dzama said hello and that he liked what I wrote to accompany his and Pettibon's work. I couldn't find Pettibon. Was he there? A crush of parka-clad gallery-goers thronged each room of the exhibition, burying the differences between them in their puffy black jackets. I had come down with a cold and felt, in my dismal state, near collapse.

Half the works were on paper, half were painted onto the walls. The gallery had invited me to see the show a few days before it was finished, while I was still working on my text for the zine, and between my preview and the opening David Bowie had died. Everyone was saying they were heartbroken, and I was heartbroken, too. In the days after I first saw the unfinished show, Dzama and Pettibon added a few works featuring the singer's different stage personas, each with titles referring to Bowie albums and songs: *Beware Diamond Dog*, 2016, and *The Supermen would walk in flames*, 2016—a misquote of Bowie's otherworldly "The Supermen" from *The Man Who Sold the World*.

Dzama has soft, warm eyes, with a bushy, inquisitive brow, and he speaks with the patience of someone who lives among restless children. "We're going ice-skating afterwards," he said, but I wasn't sure I could manage the rink. I swayed. Someone said, "Can you believe David Bowie's dead?" No, I couldn't.

WEIRA [*quietly hums "Life on Mars."*]

I made my way through the crowd a few more times, sniffling loudly as I bounced against the ice-slick surface of airy jackets. Pettibon was nowhere to be found. Then, as I was leaving, I caught him standing in the corner of the room, with a few of his friends. He didn't seem pleased to be there, but I wondered if he was ever pleased to be anywhere with such a big crowd.

WEIRA [*singing*]: "See the mice in their million hordes."

Is there life on Mars?

Or rather, he appeared uneasy with the idea of a public, as if it were a confusing and yet wonderful thing to have, all these *interested* people. Perhaps he was even a little intrigued by it. I thought to say hello, this was my chance, I finally had an excuse to talk to him since I had written something for the show. A prose poem that, funnily enough, begins with a line from a Bowie song, "Big Brother": "I found the door that lets me out." Had he recognized it? Had he read it? He was solemn, an *éminence grise* before his time, as in his self-portraits: with the sad wandering eyes of someone who's not sure where to place his attention.

I sneezed—out the door. I couldn't face up to him.

WEIRA [*singing*]: "Oh man, wonder if he'll ever know he's in the bestselling show."

The second time we met was in February 2017, a year later: *A Pen of All Work*, a survey exhibition at the New Museum. It was the opening night and the show was over-stuffed with patrons, friends of the artist and his galleries, writers, other artists, all these recognizable faces, a sea of them. I was alone. Or, no, I was with friends, though I can't exactly remember who, probably fellow artists and poets and writers, but then I separated from them or they separated from me—

"Hi, Andrew," my friend Lucas said. He's the editor of this book. We hadn't seen each other since *Forgetting the Hand*, which he had put together. "You should meet Ray," he insisted. He led me into the next room, where Pettibon stood near an installation of his drawings of big whooping blue waves with surfers shimmying across them on their boards. The drawings—some framed, but mostly pinned to the wall—were arranged in a salon-style hang.

"Ray, I want you to meet Andrew," Lucas said.

Pettibon nodded at me.

I said, "Hi."

Pettibon said, "Hi." And then he walked out.

He was like a character from Beckett, playing a role in a story he wanted no part of, and yet there he was, a Joe or an Estragon or a Vladimir or a Krapp or even a Winnie, though less a Winnie than a Krapp, absorbing whatever it was that the people around him were saying, rewinding the tape, or the feed, in his head, for himself. Beckett is comedy without the expected cues, and that might be one way to describe Pettibon, or at least his work. That the gag leaves its audience a little nervous. I mean I'm a little nervous. That the gag isn't much of a gag, but still, the question lingers . . . Why *had* I found that funny? Or is the gag you, us?

At the New Museum, Pettibon was spotlit on a makeshift stage, one larger and less flimsy than he might have imagined for himself, since it was his first major survey exhibition. His work occupied most of the museum, with drawings—framed and unframed—covering nearly every inch of wall space. Given that it was shortly after the inauguration of Donald Truymp, his work seemed even more prescient than usual. That's the way it felt, anyway, and that's the way people talked about it. Would Truymp make an appearance, on Pettibon's walls? What would he say and do? That morning he tweeted:

Legacy means nothing 2 me. When dead yr dead.The Retrospectives or BlackFAIL flyersLOL.But Greg Ginn's been main arbiter o my Wiki 4 years.

3:36 AM – 7 Feb 2017

"BlackFAIL flyers" refers to Pettibon's well-known drawing of four black bars that serves as the symbol for the band Black Flag. It is probably his most recognizable work beside the cover of Sonic Youth's *Goo*. Greg Ginn is Black Flag's guitarist and primary songwriter, Pettibon's brother and a perpetual antagonist.

WEIRA: "Another double."

A double of sorts. Greg's also a Gemini.

11

Later that night, sometime after the opening must have ended, when presumably Pettibon was leaving the dinner the museum hosted in his honor, he published a strange tweet:

Admission: Orson Bean's emission at th'bathhouse Cleveland OH b4 Tattletales Gameshow gave me th'edge won me $2500; is tht cheating?

10:47 PM – 7 Feb 2017

Orson Bean is a minor actor (still living, but retired) who regularly appeared on the seventies game show *Tattletales*. He is better known for his role as Mr. Bevis on an episode of the first season of *The Twilight Zone*. In the episode's opening narration (used, for the first time, for Bean's character), he is introduced as "an oddball" who seems at home in Pettibon's cast of the unlucky:

> His name is James B. W. Bevis, and his tastes lean toward stuffed animals, zither music, professional football, Charles Dickens, moose heads, carnivals, dogs, children, and young ladies. Mr. Bevis is accident-prone, a little vague, a little discombooberated [*sic*], with a life that possesses all of the security of a floating crap game. But this can be said of our Mr. Bevis, without him, without his warmth, without his kindness, the world would be a considerably poorer place—albeit perhaps a little saner.

WEIRA [*considering this a moment*]: "The beautiful monsters are preoccupied with pleasures."

That's from the *Forgetting the Hand* zine. But true. Bevis is something of a premonition of that twentieth-century monster, the hippie, preoccupied with his pleasures (listed by the show's narrator), a proto-bohemian freak who breaks with the norms of adult living to do his own thing. His apartment is cluttered with knickknacks: plants, overlarge furniture, mounted heads—all of it without order or place. In the opening scene, a jittery Bevis sips tea while cleaning up after himself. He shoves newspapers under the couch and struggles to find a place for a large, empty birdcage. The mess is general and extends to his financial life, too, as we learn in the following scene, when he is fired from his job, his car is impounded for a parking infraction, and he is evicted from his apartment.

After his expulsion from the office, Bevis distracts himself with shots of whiskey at a nearby bar until he is interrupted by the appearance of his guardian angel, J. Hardy Hempstead, an Eisenhower-era equivalent to Lennon's Walrus and the Zap Comix visions of psilocybin-induced dreamlands that would turn on, tune in, and drop out the second half of the decade. True to any angelic vision, no one else can see Hempstead, who sets Bevis's life right by paying his rent and offering him a sports car on condition that he give up his eccentric taste. (Imitate my life, not my art.) They tour Bevis's new home, which Hempstead has reformed into one resembling that of his neighbors: no more dead heads slung haphazard on the walls, no more Rickenbacker car. Hempstead offers him with a convertible Austin-Healey as a gift from God. Bevis is devastated. The car is too zippy, too slick. "Mr. Bevis," the angel says, "live it up a little."

"But have you ever driven a 1924 Rickenbacker?" he says.

"My dear Bevis, I've driven a chariot with eleven horses. I'm the guy responsible for Ben-Hur winning. And the old Rickenbacker went out with the old Bevis. You're a different person. No more bow ties, no more zither music, no more Christmas carolers in the office."

(God's distaste for Christmas music goes unexplained.)

Bevis declines. If he were to agree to the angel's conditions, he would lose those things that made his life worth living, that made him uniquely himself. One imagines heaven heaved a great sigh. Hempstead consents to restore things to the way they were, though, in a moment of pity, he magically returns the impounded Rickenbacker to Bevis. He finds it parked illegally in front of a fire hydrant outside the bar, with a meter cop writing out a ticket. "Your car, mister?" the cop asks.

"Well, uh."

"In this town, we take a dim view of parking in front of a hydrant." At this, the hydrant vanishes and reappears next to the police officer's motorcycle.

Bevis smiles and gets into his car: "Still with me, Mr. Hempstead?"

The voice of the angel echoes from the sky: "Still with you, Mr. Bevis. Still with you." The narrator concludes the episode:

> Mr. James B. W. Bevis, who believes in a magic all his own: a magic of a child's smile, the magic of liking and being liked, the strange and wondrous mysticism that is the simple act of living. Mr. James B. W. Bevis: specie of twentieth century male, who has his own private end special of *The Twilight Zone*.

We might see Pettibon's tweet about Orson Bean, who played Bevis, as illustrative of the artist's interest in the double and the contradictory nature of the entertainment sector in American culture, yet another curious *emission* of the boob tube's cultural gas into living rooms across the country. The figure of James B. W. Bevis is emblematic of the protagonists who fascinate Pettibon: men and women (baseball players and athletes, actors, serial killers, hippies, mothers and fathers, lovers, to name a few) who, while different in their respective motives and desires, share a common identity as people in a near-cosmic struggle to belong to the world, and who face a choice between accepting social norms or finding their own terrible path. Many of Pettibon's protagonists are marked by a condition of misplacement through which they become aware of their incompatibility with their environment. Some of these figures—like Charles Manson, who appears frequently in the drawings—leverage this condition to sinister, violent effect, seeking to have the world changed to suit their desires; others are bugged, saddened, horrified by it, finding themselves fatally detached from a world they desperately seek to join. In *No Title (Life at these . . .)*, 1989, a glowing, naked man—a superman?—stands in a cave, facing away from the viewer. Above him, Pettibon wrote:

LIFE AT THESE INTENSITIES CLEARLY BECAME 'SCENES.' WAITING TO BE DISCOVERED.

And below:

CAN I MAKE IT ON THIS EARTH?

Pettibon lived in Los Angeles for much of his life. The upside-down world of the Hollywood actor, who is both a character and him- or herself, particularly the second- or third-string actor of weird TV (game shows and other black-and-white arcana of the small screen), has long preoccupied him, from morally bankrupt iterations of Batman and Robin, each floundering in a moody turpitude of loneliness and betrayal, to various golden-era actors and celebs, like the psychically dismayed Joan Crawford and late, misty-eyed Elvis.

Pettibon's film star subjects—*the* singular "specie of [the] twentieth century"—are each haunted by the terrifying contradictions which drive their lives on and off screen. Bean is at once a homely guest on game shows, best known for a role in which he rescinds the material offerings of a god to live an impoverished but truer life, and also a creepy cheat in a Cleveland bathroom selling quiz show answers. This could possibly be a reference to the quiz show scandals of the fifties and, perhaps, the infamous cheater Michael Larson, who was from Ohio. (As far as I can tell, there's nothing on Bean selling answers.)

12

No Title (When they meet . . .), 2001, one of Pettibon's Batman drawings, bores down into this discrepancy between outward appearances and what lies beneath. In the drawing, Batman and Superman embrace in a moment of comradery, lit by a white moon in the inky night. Pettibon writes:

WHEN THEY MEET (OVER A CLARK KENT BYLINE) THE TWO SEEM ALIKE, AND PROBABLY ONE WOULD CALL THEIR SCENES A 'DECOMPOSITION' OF ONE PERSON.

THE PAPERS FALSIFIED HISTORY TO MAKE THE TWO SPLENDID CREATURES THE SAME AND REFRAIN FROM KILLING EACH OTHER.

THE FORCE AND IRONY OF THE THING DEPENDS ON MAKING US SYMPATHIZE WITH BOTH SIDES SO THAT WE ARE BAFFLED WHEN THEY MEET; THIS MAKES AN UNMANAGEABLE PLAY. LET LOOSE BY THE DOUBLE PLOT, THE PARTS TEND TO SEPARATE.

BATMAN WONDERED HOW LONG IT WOULD BE BEFORE HE COULD ASK SUPERMAN FOR FAVORS. MONEY WOULD NOT COUNT THERE, BUT POWER, *SUPER* POWER.

Batman and Superman have always been viewed in inverse relation to one another, with the Dark Knight serving as the brooding, all-too-human billionaire, pushed into vigilante justice by a sense that he's been wronged in a way money can't make right. Superman, on the other hand, isn't human at all, but insofar as he appears to us as human, he's the all-American, a Midwesterner, raised by down-home foster parents, who got an honest job in the big city as a reporter and who, when he reveals his true self as a flying alien from deep space, only strives to do good, vowing never to kill. In Frank Miller's celebrated

Dark Knight Returns, Batman's a fanatic from Gotham's pitted depths who obsesses over Superman before resolving to murder him with a kryptonite-tipped arrow. But killing Superman kills Batman: he keels over after his rampage against the son of Jor-El from a heart attack in Crime Alley, where his parents were murdered decades prior, finally broken and penniless.

Pettibon notes that every comic book or filmic meeting of Batman and Superman baffles us. We are invited to consider them as opposites, as incompatible forces that cancel one another out but who are nevertheless kindred spirits—or beasts: superficially different, but structurally occupying the same place within an imagined sphere of power, with one serving (and standing in for) the day and the other the night. They are monsters, mutated figures from everyday life—the rich heir and the reporter—who possess and are possessed by powers that elevate and ultimately destroy them. This is what makes any monster so alluring, for their terrible face doubles as a glassy mask that reflects our own while simultaneously embodying something of its antithesis, an embodiment that is at once horrifying and deeply recognizable, and therefore wickedly attractive.

WEIRA [*mournfully*]: "The once-beautiful Medusa. The head Perseus must take."

Or, later, Mary Shelley's monster, whom Dr. Frankenstein encounters in a window after he has dreamt of beholding his dear Elizabeth "in the bloom of health," her lips pursed to receive his. He stirs as her creaturely opposite emerges out of the dream and into real life:

> Delighted and surprised, I embraced her, but as I imprinted the first kiss on her lips, they became livid with the hue of death; her features appeared to change, and I thought that I held the corpse of my dead mother in my arms; a shroud enveloped her form, and I saw the grave-worms crawling in the folds of the flannel. I started from my sleep with horror; a cold dew covered my

forehead, my teeth chattered, and every limb became convulsed; when, by the dim and yellow light of the moon, as it forced its way through the window shutters, I beheld the wretch—the miserable monster whom I had created. He held up the curtain of the bed; and his eyes, if eyes they may be called, were fixed on me. His jaws opened, and he muttered some inarticulate sounds, while a grin wrinkled his cheeks. [. . .] Oh! No mortal could support the horror of that countenance. A mummy again endued with animation could not be so hideous as that wretch. I had gazed on him while unfinished; he was ugly then, but when those muscles and joints were rendered capable of motion, it became a thing such as even Dante could not have conceived.

Batman and Superman "decompose" into one another, to use Pettibon's term, and are frightened of their uncanny similarity, like the deformed face that transposes itself onto the doctor's dream of Elizabeth and his dead mother. It is this decomposition—the erosion of known and perceived boundaries—between antitheses, contradictory doubles, twins, real life and dream that animates the illimitable anxiety that pervades Pettibon's work. The encounter with the inverse always threatens to undermine the division that keeps the self whole, and not a hole.

WEIRA: "George W. Batman."

These beasts come from dreams, from the rooms hidden within dreams, secret places we don't dare remember when we wake. But most often they come from Yale. And that is Pettibon's point: that behind the unreal face of power is always a real one. Under the bat, Bruce Wayne, businessman and philanthropist. Wealth and power strive to clean up the seams around the mask; Pettibon, on the other hand, seeks to tear the mask off, to expose not only its artifice and the face behind it, but the hands that fashioned it, too. He exposes the beastliness that eats through one's humanity, from the inside out, what William S.

Burroughs once referred to as "the policeman within." *No Title (Which side of. . .)*, 1982: a long-haired man dressed in plaid is being led away by officers. Pettibon writes:

WHICH SIDE OF HIM MURDERED (46 GIRLS): THE CRAZED HIPPIE OR THE NORMAL ONE?

Pettibon has a lighter touch, too. To return to those "beautiful monsters" in the *Forgetting the Hand* zine and exhibition, each drawing is a blend of Dzama and Pettibon, where the distinction between artists is blurred—or forgotten. In their collaboration, Dzama imitated Pettibon and Pettibon imitated Dzama, so that each work muddies the viewer's understanding of who did what. Instead, their respective styles decompose into a corpus of scrambled parts.

[WEIRA *opens her copy of the zine and lays it out in front of* THE WRITER. *She flips through a few pages and settles on one.*]

The drawing shows a woman with a bow. Her taut arrow points at two embracing lovers. Below them, three naked men appear to be cruising one another. The text reads:

FACTS WERE FOR BENDING.

Are the lovers Pettibon's? They look like his, but I suspect they are Dzama's.

[THE WRITER and WIERA *continue to look through the zine together. She stops at* THE WRITER's *contribution. She begins to read it aloud. He stops her out of embarrassment.*]

WIERA: "You never mentioned the third time you saw him."

I saw him for the third time, briefly, at his exhibition *TH' EXPO-SIYV SHOYRT T* (WEIRA: "Is that T for twiyt?"), which was held in David Zwirner's garage-like gallery on 19th Street in 2017. I had come early, there were only a few people at the opening at that point, but Pettibon stood alone in the corner, beneath a drawing of a giggling skull observing a buck with a tree branch posed atop its head:

I LOVE HONEST LAUGHTER, AS I DO SUNLIGHT.
SUCH GRINNING INSANITY IS VERY SAD TO THE SOUL OF MAN.

13

We might view Pettibon's Twitter as he sees Art Clokely's Gumby, a bendable character from fifties television, who has appeared in the drawings since the 1980s, and whose elasticity Pettibon closely associates with the fickle nature of art, especially literary art. Gumby encounters works and is shaped, even consumed by them. Gumby-Ray, phone in hand, bends to (and absorbs) notions of bad and good by incorporating them into his feed in highly dramatic or provocative ways. In a 1998 work Pettibon writes:

FAITHFUL TO TRUTH, BUT EVEN MORE SO TO PLAY-DO™,* THE FRIEND THAT HE IS.

The asterisk leads us to:

OR, AS GUMBY™ CALLS HIM, PLATO.

And this fealty to the "play-do" of art rather than objective truth holds throughout the Gumby drawings. In *No Title (You thought this . . .)*, 2005, Gumby stretches wildly into a web of green limbs that enclose a fleeing figure (the artist? the viewer?) Pettibon writes at the top:

YOU THOUGHT THIS WAS GOING TO BE ART.

Below:

IT *IS* ART.

In *No Title (Then he began . . .)*, 1990, Gumby stares at Flaubert's *Madame Bovary*. Pettibon writes, in his pristine, controlled cursive, of the reader's self-negation in the face of the book (and, for our purposes, let's say Twitter):

Then he began to feel that his own life was drifting into the all-absorbing work, that his own soul was entering, gumdrop by gumdrop, into the person of the drama, that his aspects, his attitudes, his gestures, and his accents were contributing to the formation of the figure of the heroine 'living beyond life.'

The image of one's soul being pulled (and, in variance with the drawing, lost), gumdrop by gumdrop, into the person of the drama, into the feed, into all those consuming voices, White House correspondents, *InfoWars* trolls, porn stars, artists, superfans, Black Twitter, Gay Twitter, "influencers," is recognizable to most Twitter users. A twiyt goes beyond life.

14

I first wanted to understand Pettibon's Twitter when I became interested in his use of the letter Y. Since the 2000s, the letter has gone viral in his work—cutting into, splitting, and altering words in a way that complicates and slows down the reader. I once thought the Y was an effort to increase linguistic redundancy in his work and make things wordier, calling our attention to words as things and to the relative arbitrariness of those things. The Y is originally a Greek letter that Latin cribbed when it needed to accommodate a Hellenic lingo, and it has never had an easy time in the Romance languages, ever playing the foreigner to the colder tongues of western and northern Europe (most languages refer to the letter's Greek origins: *i grec* in French, for example, or *i griega* in Spanish). In English, it serves uniquely as both a vowel and consonant.

Lately, I've come to see a more literal side of the Y: that it acts as a tripwire in Pettibon's logic, a coded expression of self-doubt: *why?*

WEIRA: "Whyyhyhyhyyyyy."

See his 2009 video collaboration with Yoshua Okón, *Hipnostasis*. The film is about hippies on the beach, and its title conflates hippie, hypnosis (to lose the Y!), and hypostasis—the underlying substance of the world—into a neologism to describe beach-bum reality. Hypostasis relates to literature, too, something Pettibon cares deeply about, if not for its terminology than for its works and workers. A hypostatic moment is the odd instance in a work of literature where a character becomes aware that he, she, or it is a creation in a book. You might read Pettibon's Y as a hypostatic moment on the non-narrative level of the word, wherein a word becomes aware of itself as a word and asks, Y?

There is an almost unbearable degree of self-consciousness to Pettibon and his work. That's the Y, the whyhyhy.

WEIRA: "Us, I suppose. Or me here. Y: Whyhy. I guess I always had myself pegged as a fake."

A fiction. Does your self-awareness—or my construction of your self-awareness—screw with our thing?

WEIRA [*sighing*]: "Naturally. It ends it. For now. Buh-bye, my writer. He's all yours."

[*She retreats into smoke.*]

15

[THE WRITER *is left standing alone before a gray door with a number on it, the number doesn't matter nor does the precise location of the room, though it is a real place, down on Broadway in Lower Manhattan. He knocks several times but no one answers. He paces the landing a few times, knocks again, a little harder, but still no one answers. He begins to walk down the stairs, having given up (he's surprised to find himself tired and mildly hungover), but then he pauses on the ground floor, walks back up to the door, and bangs as hard as he can. Finally, a young man—*THE ASSISTANT *to* RAYMOND PETTIBON—*answers.*]

THE ASSISTANT: "Hey, come in. Sorry, we didn't hear you."

16

Lodged in an unassuming building in the much-trafficked center of SoHo, Raymond Pettibon's studio is long and wide, with dim overhead light. A narrow, book-crammed hallway extends roughly twelve feet before opening into the vast main workspace, where a small kitchen hugs the right wall at the start of the central room. Drawings lie in stacks on a row of tables lining the left side of the studio. Modest dime-store paintings and original works by Margaret Keane (known for her "big eyes" paintings from the sixties) lean on a built-in shelf just below the high ceiling, a little out of view unless you look up. Framed vintage posters of baseball players hang on the wall near the entrance, as does a portrait of Pettibon's uncle, who was a Catholic priest and friend of Ad Reinhardt at Columbia University. The room is well-kept, since it is too large and appears too new for the space to have accumulated the usual grime (no stale air of the decades-old studio). Also, the presence of the assistant, who greeted me with the mildly authoritative attitude of a sergeant-at-arms, suggests that there are forces beyond the artist at work to organize the teeming scrawl.

Pettibon stands near the kitchen island with his back to me. He is silent. I had suspected that our first real meeting would be uncomfortable, or at least marked by the weird artificiality that complicates any author–subject relationship, but now, as I make small talk with the assistant and Pettibon continues to loiter at a remove, turning only to smile faintly at me before looking coolly into the distance over my head as I explain what I'm doing ("writing a book about Ray's, um, Twitter"), I wonder if this is a mistake, if his and my anxiety will get the better of us.

Should I have not come to his studio and instead developed an image of him through his Twitter account rather than from knowing him in person, as had been my original plan? Will I get a word out of him? My purpose makes me feel out of place: I'm play-acting the journalist, here to ferret out an idea of a subject that will suit my work, the story I'm trying to tell, a story that every subject seeks, in his own way, to resist or control. In response to this complex game between author and subject, a mild guilt attaches itself to our interaction: I'm here to take something away and make of it a book—of Pettibon on Twitter, of Pettibon as writer-artist. Which, at least, interests both of us. Writing, that is.

THE WRITER [*to* THE ASSISTANT]: "Thanks for having me over."

The air conditioner purrs. I've had too much coffee, and one too many drinks the night before. I gulp and walk over to Pettibon, who remains in the kitchen. Each step toward him requires an extra-long stride as I bridge the yawning distance between us. When I finally arrive at him, in the great big room where he makes his art, he nods. I say I'm the writer, THE WRITER, here to talk about Twitter, awful as it is to say aloud. The platform's name sticks in my throat: there is something unseemly about discussing social media in person, as if our internet-selves ought to remain unbothered in their digital underworld, beasts apart. To give it place in conversation feels like an undressing in public.

THE WRITER: "So. Twitter."

17

I am struck by his face, which I know best from his own drawings of it. He has soft, plain eyes, tangled gray hair, a small, quivering mouth. He is somewhat blank in person, by which I mean he seems to have guarded himself against the invasive outside that I, in this case, represent. Or he's simply nervous, stalled iyn a momynt of Y. I reach into my bag to retrieve a new book by the San Francisco-based poet Kevin Killian, a mutual friend, in hopes that it might spark a feeling of community between us, of belonging, however distantly, to the same crowd. I suspect he doesn't have a copy yet and I'm right. "He's a friend of mine," I say, handing him the new book. Pettibon, RAYMOND PETTIBON, nods in agreement. He says that he likes Kevin's poetry. He is friends with Kevin's partner, too, the poet, essayist, and novelist Dodie Bellamy.

I want to say: "They introduced me to your work, years ago, in San Francisco. I've thought about it ever since." Instead, I look around and think: *What next?*

RAYMOND PETTIBON: "You want anything to eat or drink?"

THE WRITER [*shakes his head no*]: "But thank you."

We take a seat at a small table near the front of the room. I think to move quickly to the point: that I'm here to talk about his use of Twitter, and not slip into vague pleasantries. *Why exactly am I at his studio? I tell myself: You're writing a book on his Twitter. Do I say what that looks like, how it sounds, what argument I'm attempting to make, and why? I think: No, you're writing a book about the person who tweets as @raymondpettibon. Does he know? Does he care?* It is midsummer, probably the hottest week of the year; nobody knows anything on days like this, nor do they care. Or this isn't really true—and I imagine that, in his way, he knows, he cares, despite the distending summer heat that has left most of the city brain-dead. I open the app I use to record interviews, set my phone beside Pettibon, and rush out, "You started Twitter in 2011, so I'm curious what made you get one?"

I know what I want him to say and I know, as soon as he begins to consider the question, that he will not come close to saying it.

He stares ahead.

[*A long pause.*]

Begin with the basics, I had thought. As the moment drags past the twenty-second mark, I begin to think I've made a mistake, he might not say anything at all, it's taking too long for him to answer the question for it to be good or of any use to him or me. I think: *Have I misfired?* Also: *Calm down.* And: *Be patient.*

RAYMOND PETTIBON: "I came to computers late . . . and, then, Twitter I didn't understand at all. I thought it was very odd that people would be checking in all hours of the day, you know, making a note of what they do as they do it, before they do it, or as an afterthought. It's like making a record of everything rather than living your life."

THE WRITER: "Do you see it as a diaristic project?"

[*Another long pause.*]

RAYMOND PETTIBON: "In my case, not so much—not as a true confessional, diaristic . . . that's not . . . my art has never been that personal to begin with. It may use those techniques or those forms or presentation, but I can't say it's, you know, truly from the heart or even off the cuff. It's rather more impersonal."

THE WRITER: "As someone who's watched it since you started tweeting, it seems like a way to think concisely about politics."

[*Long pause.*]

18

Concision is not the word.

Milhouse Nixon n BeBe?Well their longtime companionship ouytlasted RFK's w/Joe McC cuzz o hepatitusC.Obama's w/Bibi goin on 8yrs.Luyvfest.

4:36 AM – 10 Nov 2014

Whyno politic sabremetrics 4 politicians? Ruth hit 714 hr,BoBonds WAR.Lincoln,Wilson, FDR,JFK,LBJ,RMN,WRostow,Kissinger. HnB,OB:Killfild

1:03 AM – 19 Oct 2015

What next?

19

RAYMOND PETTIBON: "For me, it's like a signaling device. It's like wearing a political button and announcing yourself. I'm this sort of politics, I'm a good person, look at me, validate me with follows or approval or favorites, you know. And it's . . . and then it can also be contrary, curmudgeonly, to get a cheap response from it."

I ask him why he's recently been retweeting right-wing articles about a black man who claims to be Bill Clinton's son. He nods in approval. Even in person, Pettibon is conspiracy-minded, and in this he seems the most prepared to tell—or at least understand—the story of our time of roving falsehoods and secret truths. Whether the man is his son is irrelevant, he says, since a DNA test has already proven that they aren't related, but "it still says something." He allows this to settle between us. I want to push him on its logic—and to probe the border between what can be said to be "his" politics and the politics he tweets. What *does* it say, exactly? I think to counter, "Wouldn't your argument—that Bill Clinton is a predatory philanderer who should never have been allowed to assume the presidency—be better served if it was backed up by more credible, reality-oriented claims against him, or if it was framed in terms of how men *actually* abuse power, as Clinton did?" But I'm kowtowed by our face-to-face meeting, by Pettibon's solemnity, and I don't.

THE WRITER: "Okay."

The idea fades before I can take it further.

A difficulty: Pettibon is a quiet man who speaks slowly, with sustained, awkward silences between words and ideas, and our conversation lacks good rhythm; it flits and burps, stumbles about as I try to land a question or to offer an idea, a thread we might follow into the work and the Twitter. It is tougher than I had imagined. *How can I push him on Bill?* Sometimes he doesn't respond directly to my question and I have to repeat it, or he finishes a sentence and I'm not sure what to say in follow-up. *Ask him about power—but is that too broad? Narrow it down: the presidency.* His few words hang in the air. I cling to them when I can.

THE WRITER: "You write much less about the current president than Hillary and Bill."

Pettibon says he doesn't criticize Truymp online as much as he did Barack Obama or Hillary Clinton because Truymp has already reached the point of self-parody. He lays bare in every word, every action, every tweet his own absurdity. He says that it's inherent in the self-caricature of Truymp already. His rise and success confirm, with breathless theatricality, the presidency's violence, its carelessness, its danger as an institution; that beneath its historicizing romances and demagogic banalities, there is no decency to the commanding protectorate of liberal democracy—only the sham appearance of institutional niceties. Truymp adores the drama of power. The soothing, decorous aspects of the office—press shots with survivors of national tragedies, attendance at arts honors, grandiloquent speeches before hallowed national ground—mean nothing to him, and in this he reveals the presidency's true aim: to fuck shit up.

I thot I thaw a Tweeyty-Bird!----
You saw a Drone, fooyl.

4:13 AM – 26 Mar 2016

Pettibon tells me he doesn't think of his Twitter as particularly political (though politics is a major aspect of his writing on the platform), rather he turns to it "out of sheer idleness." But idleness, then, *is* a politics for Pettibon and one that I link, with some hesitation, to Truymp's own on the platform.

Both men favor the shitpost—a non-constructive, ad hominem attack on an opponent, often characterized by self-defeating or blinding anger—as a critique of the opposition, though for different purposes and to wildly different ends. Trump uses Twitter to rouse his reluctant supporters in Congress to action, to color the white cheeks of his voters with the blush of anger, and despite his rambling style, his desire is always to make himself clear and comprehensible (in both his explicit and coded speech). He wants things, specific things done: FBI agents fired, political opponents jailed. His shitposts are designed to read as funny to his right-wing supporters, as moments of lightness in the otherwise panicked stream of his daily tweets, and their point, however confused, remains their legibility to a target audience. Pettibon, on the other hand, routes language—some of it possibly recognizable to those same supporters of Truymp—through his own unique idiolect, and a shitpost in a private language is hardly retweetable.

I'm officially dating Taylor Swift. Sorry,
Kanye; don't like it uyp the ass...Is tht wrong?
Cuzz I like him A LOYT!

1:49 AM – 26 Mar 2013

Truymp rose to power through the casual shitpost, from his alignment with the birther movement to his 2016 presidential campaign, and he continues to make use of it as President. On August 24, 2017, three days after a total eclipse of the sun was visible across much of the US, Truymp retweeted a meme posted by a reportedly anti-Semitic user named @JerryTravone. The image is divided into four quadrants, each with the same black-and-white photograph of Barack Obama. From quadrant one to four, a grinning, color image of Donald Truymp slowly moves across Obama to block him out. Below, the caption reads:

THE BEST ECLIPSE EVER!

The meme is a classic Truympian shitpost: it is vindictive on personal, racialized terms and, moreover, it is, by its own logic, a self-defeating critique since its equation of Obama with the sun and Truymp with the moon analogizes his target as the bright heavenly body that all life on earth draws upon to survive and himself as only a temporary courier of darkness. In the Truymp-eclipse, it is Truymp who lasts for only a few minutes before the light of his predecessor returns. (The metaphor is richer when one considers that the moon is visible only because it coldly reflects the light of the sun and would otherwise be largely invisible from earth.)

Twitter lends itself to the shitpost and, in many ways, it is a tweet's ideal form: brief and instantly shareable, it's a linguistic middle finger to the world, one that should receive no response because no response is necessary. Disapproving retorts find themselves relegated to a one-click-removed dropdown list appended to the tweet. And if it's an image, all the better, for it can travel across platforms—a meager but rangy beast of mean ambition. The shitpost, insofar as it represents a viable politics (and Truymp's success suggests it does), is the most effective signal one's twiyt device can transmit to the world. And when enough of them are sent, elections can be won. Much was made of "fake news" after the 2016 election, carried across the web by malicious bots, but in fact a great deal of what was shared—by real people and the fake—were canny shitposts that deftly undercut Clinton's appeal, especially when Truymp picked them up and boosted their signal: Was she a closeted lesbian? Secretly ill? Did she have a body double? Was her entire life and career a mere cover for a sexual predator? And did she, in fact, run a child sex ring out of a pizza restaurant in the capital?

Pettibon's shitposts seldom use images. Rather they take the form of rough-edged, Y-ridden attacks, but their logic is private and overextended, a little confusing, even goofy:

The face o USSA Amerikka th'Pornstar Hulk Hogan

6:50 PM – 8 Apr 2016

20

RAYMOND PETTIBON: "It's like in wrestling, [you get] to be a good guy or a bad guy."

Sports, including wrestling, have been a significant theme in Pettibon's work for several decades. Wrestlers, as both performers and as men of strength, express a complex masculine sexuality in the drawings, both in their drive to dominate fellow men and their hunky melodrama that inevitably suggests a homosexual erotics, a subject Pettibon has persistently flirted with throughout his career (see, for example, his naked baseball players, or the cover of *Homo Americanus*, which features a punk rocker with a rainbow Mohawk and a Black Flag T-shirt with its logo colorized to suggest the LGBTQ flag).

In *No Title (While we are . . .)*, 2001, three men have wrestled one another to the ground, their naked bodies fleshed out in thatched pen marks that emphasize their buttocks, foregrounding the classicism of the sport while attending to the casual sexuality of their threesome. Pettibon writes above one:

**WERE THEY NOT NOBLE?
MODELS OF HUMAN BEAUTY MADE
HERE, OUTLINED AGAINST THE SEA,
LIKE STATUES FROLICKING IN
THE SUNLIGHT UPON A GRECIAN SHORE?**

And at the top of the drawing:

**WHILE WE ARE CONSIDERING THE VERY
BEST POSSIBLE HOLD ON AN OBJECT OF
DESIRE, WE FIND THAT IT HAS SLIPPED
THROUGH OUR FINGERS**

As objects of desire repeatedly slip out of the hands of Pettibon's splenetic protagonists, many of whom endeavor to understand why they desired something in the first place (or were themselves desired, for that matter), Pettibon's athletes offer a unique, almost glorious set of relations to the strained and desperate reality his work captures: their physical struggle occurs within the existing framework of the game in which the desired outcome—triumph, say—is bound safely to its loss. It is this condition of human play that Pettibon seems to valorize as both right and properly limited, even if the tragic world outside the game intervenes (or is "interwoven," as he writes of a player's alcoholism in *No Title (Our hero's alcoholism . . .)*, 1987).

This is quite different from his typical subjects, who are often at the violent or confused whims of others, swirling in the random course of human events, where borders shift or disappear and all limits are removed or superseded by the power relations that determine our place in the world. Pettibon's protagonists cannot seem to contain their wants and needs, and so they seek to bend the world to meet them and, in doing so, inevitably find themselves bent by it. Sports, on the other hand, offer an idealized format for the expression of desire and its loss, since its stakes are preset at an acceptable level determined by the rules of the game. Frequently, baseball players are lone figures on the paper, with the world slipping away, as in *No Title (Of a bow . . .)*, 1991:

**MY STRONGEST AFFINITY
IN THE MATTER OF SUBJECT:
HOME PLATE . . . THE STILL-LIFE
AT THE HUB . . . I COULD PAINT
ITS CORNERS ALL GAME FOR STRIKES
AND NEVER NEED THE WHITE-WASH.
EACH PITCH LIKE A LETTER FROM A PERSON
TO A PLACE ABOUT A THING: ADDRESSED
TO NO ONE--THE BATTER DOESN'T
COUNT (STRIKE THREE!)--RETURN TO
SENDER.
IN THE PERFECT GAME THE BATTER IS
ALL BUT NOT THERE.**

Both the player and the outside world dissolve *into the tightly controlled economy of the game*—and this image, in many ways, reverses Twitter's riot of individuals. While sports exist in a reality seemingly parallel to our own, wherein the rule-bound competition of bodies allows for a meaningful freedom from the outside, Twitter's own parallel reality brings about an endless competition of voices that fails to allow for any freedom at all, it would seem, and instead mires its users in memes and disinformation.

21

Pettibon sips his Gatorade and asks me again if I want one, perhaps sensing that the going is rough for me, that I'm nervous in his presence. It's an ordinary kindness that's somehow invested with supernatural meaning for me, the simple offering of a drink—and Pettibon's potential recognition, in me, of the need for one—when I'm a stranger. I think: *Say yes to the Gatorade.* Then: *No.* Then: *Maybe.* Then: *No.*

THE WRITER: "Thanks, but I'm all right."

[A loud fan blows. Two people enter the studio: they are actors in RAY-MOND PETTIBON's new film. They begin to set up at a nearby table for a later run-through of the film script. They greet the artist and THE WRITER before sitting down to quietly read over their lines before practice. RAYMOND PETTIBON says he needs to step away to speak with them. They huddle for a few minutes to discuss the film. Everyone agrees to something. Papers are exchanged. Rehearsal begins and RAYMOND PETTIBON returns with a cigar. He chews the stub as he lights the cigar's end, puffs once or twice, then sets it down on a small ash tray.]

THE WRITER: "Is it a tool for provocation?"

RAYMOND PETTIBON: "Yeah, at times . . ."

Inspired by the cigar, I circle back to his criticism of Bill and Hillary and to whether he sees his shitposting (I don't use that word and instead call it "critique") as fitting with his career-long critical commentary on power.

RAYMOND PETTIBON: "Yeah, well, bypassing Hillary, if you look at Obama, that was eight years of basically another George W. Bush, with a benign, happy face. And having him in office wiped off all dissent on the face of the earth. Every anti-war sentiment was in limbo for eight years. In that respect, that's more what I mean. To me it's more important to criticize the people who you are closest to in a way. That you have a voice toward. To be able to nudge them or put them on the right track. Mind you this is all spoken with the acknowledgment that I have absolutely no power as an artist or as someone with a Twitter account."

22

It is the dead of summer—a Nazi summer of white power demonstrations around the country, of immigrant-taunting, and mosque burnings. Truymp's fingers are never far from his Twitter, and white supremacists have clogged the feed with their eugenicist screeds. The app feels lost to those of us who use it; Twitter has been seized by the very bad actors we were promised had been blocked or removed, who only a few years ago were under close watch by the Southern Poverty Law Center and the Justice Department. Everyone is discussing Twitter because of its most famous user. The air is choked with the dishonesty of his opinions, issued in 140-character missives in the early morning, later to be gussied up as policy and fact. Pettibon and I have sputtered along for about thirty minutes, though much of the conversation has been filled with his silence.

THE WRITER: "What do you think about how popular Twitter has become with Nazis?"

[RAYMOND PETTIBON *shrugs his shoulders.*]

At the top of its homepage, Twitter poses the question: What's happening? In the studio, there are many long pauses as I ask about the differences between various platforms, if Pettibon see his Twitter as an extension of his art—

RAYMOND PETTIBON: "I've had thoughts that I would like them to, uh, configure, you know, to make a [*inaudible*] . . . to where, someday the Twitter will be, will be doing the same thing I make art for. Not that it has to be, not that one has to be replaced or not, but . . . to make those the way I would make artwork."

[*Long pause.*]

—but we get nowhere, or at least not to any point . . . of revelation? Of [*inaudible*]? Twitter might serve as an art but doesn't, he says. But he says the opposite, too. He hasn't decided.

[*Long pause.*]

The problem between us seems to be a journalistic one, since any good journalist could capture, in the conversational sparring that marks his or her summit with a subject, the story, or I'm not a good journalist, or that the story

[*Long pause.*]

is not here, in our conversation about the social media platform. Pettibon slips past me

[*Long pause.*]

into silence.

The writer Janet Malcolm has dwelled upon the thorny issue of the subject–journalist relationship for much of her career. In *The Silent Woman*, her book on the biographers of Sylvia Plath and the wily, insuperable nature of writing about other people, she considers Borges's story "The Aleph" and converts its indescribable subject—"an iridescent sphere of almost unbearable brilliance" that contains "infinite things"—into a metaphor for biography. In dying, Plath provided such an object—her life—to the people who have attempted to account for it, one that has managed to suggest, in the posthumous vagaries of a written life, every conceivable reading of every line, incident, rumor, diary entry, letter, friend or foe account. This proved to be an unbearable object for the living who inherited it (Ted Hughes, Olwyn Hughes, Plath's mother) and those who have attempted to take it for themselves, to do something with it, to search in Plath's aleph for some truth.

In Borges's story, the narrator sees everything in the aleph "from every angle of the universe":

I saw the teeming sea; I saw daybreak and nightfall; I saw the multitudes of America; I saw a silvery cobweb in the center of a black pyramid; I saw a splintered labyrinth (it was London); I saw, up close, unending eyes watching themselves in me as in a mirror; I saw all the mirrors on earth and none of them reflected me; I saw in a backyard of Soler Street the same tiles that thirty years before

I'd seen in the entrance of a house in Fray Bentos; I saw bunches of grapes, snow, tobacco, lodes of metal, steam; I saw convex equatorial deserts and and each one of their grains of sand [. . .]

And in the aleph I can see, as Malcolm saw, a metaphor for my subject—Pettibon. Within his work, Twitter included, one can list, as Borges's narrator does, a seemingly endless amount of stuff of the known world, all its glories and agonies, pretty things and false ones, too, the good guy and the bad, Superman and Batman, Gumby and Truymp. To make a description of it—to fashion an argument about the use of language—has left me, in the moment of conversing with Pettibon, overwhelmed, as Borges's narrator was when he finally saw the incredible object himself.

WEIRA [*from above*]: "He almost couldn't believe it, right? But Ray? Anyone can believe in him, in his work: it's all there, too."

Are you back?

WEIRA [*from above*]: "Comin' now."

As Pettibon speaks, I make a list of things I see within his aleph, an incomplete inventory of his subjects:

baseball players
waves, surfers
Gumby, Superman, Manson
America
"America's enemies"
bombs, rockets, missiles
lovers
addiction, drugs
music
monsters
generals, soldiers
dictators, presidents, politicians

lies, truth
faithlessness
small talk, silence
interiority
the fake
convex equatorial personalities and each of their
thoughts, emotions

23

"I am a natural reader, and only a writer in the absence of natural writers. In a true time, I should never have written."—Sincerely, Ray

2:26 PM – 18 Jan 2013

24

[Long pause, and within it:]

WEIRA [*returning*]: "Leyt's take a slight detour to gin you uyp t' energy to geyt this thing done. Do you know the drawings he's made of the mushroom cloud? There are many."

Not unlike his waves, the clouds build in furious, curved pen strokes as surrounding landscapes and suburban vistas shatter before their awesome power. The accompanying text is often nightmarish, as Pettibon emphasizes the stark ironies of advanced civilization's singular weapon, our Sword of Damocles clamoring in the sky. In *No Title (I have made . . .)*, 2007, an atomic bomb rises in blue-green gouache and acrylic on paper. Written above the cloud's cresting dome:

I HAVE MADE IT LARGE, IN HOPE THAT YOU NOTICE IT

Below:

NOW WHAT WILL YOU DO WITH IT?

And in *No Title (When I see . . .)*, 2006, a frantic, text-heavy pen-and-ink drawing with collage, Shriners, protesters, clowns, civilians scramble in the fallout of a nuclear bomb. The mushroom cloud reads:

SO MUCH IS EPHEMERAL TO THIS WORLD, THAT WE'LL HARDLY NOTICE WHEN IT DISAPPEARS.

Fck em all.Bomb,Bomb : cauliflowered eared mushroom cloud is enuff shock n awe for any of us.N xclamation point on myTHE END!

11:03 PM – 6 Oct 2014

WEIRA: "Such destruction terrifies you as it does because through it, through the bomb, you can finally conceive of the end of yourselves. Remember when it was MAD that kept you afloat?"

We've dropped like lead.

WEIRA: "It's so pretty to those who keep them as pets. It seems that the idea of destroying yourselves gives you, like, a total boner."

Where are we going with this?

WEIRA: "Paytience! After its 'successful' use, first at Trinity and then later at Nagasaki and Hiroshima, the bomb brought about a new world, the atomic age, while coding midcentury optimism with the possibility of its immediate annihilation. And with that annihilation, a renewed possibility of silence, real and imagined. The silence of history, as we lesser angels are blown back by its winds. The world's end is always accompanied by *silence*, a loss of words, the end of speech. Last men and women, or none at all. Imagine a thing more contra Ray? Think of his drawing of an eye, widening in shock, for his 2013 Rizzoli catalog, above which he wrote:

I AM STRUCK ALMOST INTO SILENCE.

What is reflected in that eye?"

Almost, but never completely, never fully. In that eye, a wan reality: darkness. Pettibon resists the temptation to quiet down, to let words fail in the fallout. He is *against* the sublime quality of human and natural things, really, and nothing is too big to fit into one's mouth.

The resistance to silence is almost an anti-modernist kind of thing (*pace* Wittgenstein: "What we cannot speak of we must pass over in silence"), when silence was made art's starkest prerogative (Cage, of course, but even Reinhardt's shift from comics to black paintings). Not Pettibon, who greets the quiet with gab; he is fueled by speech, by the gut-deep drive to make a racket, to Make It Purple, if not New.

WEIRA: "Reinhardt's not quite silent. At the end, he published his list of 'no' demands, *No War*, 1967, in opposition to the Vietnam War:

NO WAR

NO IMPERIALISM

NO MURDER

NO BOMBINGS

NO NAPALM

NO ESCALATION

NO CREDIBILITY GAP

NO PROPAGANDA

NO BULLSHIT

NO LYING

NO IGNORANCE

NO GRAFT

NO POVERTY

NO HUNGER

NO HATE

NO INJUSTICE

NO EVIL

NO INHUMANITY

NO CALLOUSNESS

NO CONSIOUSLESSNESS

NO CONSCIENCELESSNESS

NO ART OF WAR

NO ART IN WAR

NO ART TO WAR

NO ART ON WAR

NO ART BY WAR

NO ART ABOUT WAR

NO ART FOR WAR

NO ART WITH WAR

NO ART AS WAR

And then he was done."

Fuck what we cannot speak of, Pettibon says, there will be no passing over anything in silence. Let's see it, and let's speak of it. He might add (I might add):

NO SILENCE

25

WEIRA: "La tristesse durera toujours, sweetums."

In *No Title (I have had . . .)*, 2003, the shadowy figure of a woman flees her suburb as a mushroom cloud spoils the blue sky behind her. He writes above her:

"I HAVE HAD TIME TO HEAR FROM THREE OR FOUR FRIENDS AS TO THE EFFECT OF THE THING."

And beside the bomb:

IT WILL COME WITH ITS OWN ANNOUNCEMENT—SUDDEN AND LOUD.

Below this:

TELL THE WORLD.

In *No Title (The same tragic . . .)*, 1990, he writes:

THE SAME TRAGIC THEMES MUST EXIST EVERYWHERE.

WEIRA: "Gertrude Stein said the bomb was not interesting, and therefore no one should take much interest in it because 'it's the living that are interesting not the way of killing them . . . Everybody gets so much information all day long that they lose their common sense. They listen so much that they forget to be natural.' I'd wager that the bomb helped inaugurate an era of information, the atomic age, the cap-off to the revolution started by Babbage's adding machine and Turing's test and so on, and that information is a means to *silence*, to overwhelm, to dull, for information is not knowledge, of course, and it is knowledge that one needs to think and to talk, writer, not information. Information is just facts, and facts are not thinking!! Ray's about more than facts. Maybe he hates facts, like, the Regime of Facts—the Accepted Narrative, that is."

[*A loud boom rattles* WEIRA *and* THE WRITER.]

"Let's go back to where your sex-slick death drive began: in the gaslit capitals of post-Napoleonic Europe. That's where the bomb finds its ancestral past, in the crackle of the fuse burning out and subsequent bang [*she slams her fist down on the table*] as the dynamite shatters a public square or a magistrate's parlor. The bomb is both the negation of and the realization of the nineteenth century anarchist's dream of an instantaneous weapon that might bring about a new world through its detonation. The German writer Joachim Kalka traces your society's bombs to dynamite, when a truly portable explosive thing first became possible and was quickly co-opted by anarchists and governments alike. What gets lost in the bomb is the mundanity of its origins, or the origins of the drive that drove y'all to produce it, to invent the 'bomb to end all bombs': it was once just a stick with a fuse. And it's the ordinariness of the thing that should concern us."

I had no idea you . . .

WEIRA: "That in this hairy head I've got a brain?" [THE WRITER *nods.*] "Keep up. We're near our end, so movin' on: Kalka writes of the 1883 assassination attempt on the German Kaiser and the Crown Prince at the dedication of the Niederwalddenkmal—the monument that commemorates the unification of Germany—by two anarchists using dynamite. The plot was foiled by the bomb itself: it didn't blow, and the anarchists were apprehended on site. During their trial (Kalka sources the writer Hugo Friedländer's account), the prosecution noted that anarchists transported the dynamite in a stoneware pot, which they rigged to ignite when a lit cigar brushed its fuse. One of the co-defendants insisted that he had *thwarted* the attempted assassination by using an extinguished cigar, to which the Court replied, in terms that Ray might crib for a joke, 'So with your cold cigar you blackened the fuse of a dynamite, in consequence of which the explosion did not take place?'—*TH' EXPOSIYV SHOYRT T.* Kalka writes: 'the act of smoking lends a mysteriously casual touch to the fatal hand motion.' The jury bought the argument, and one of the conspirators was let off the hook while the other was executed."

When Pettibon set his cigar down in our conversation, I asked him if he enjoyed them often. "Rarely," he said. I didn't know what the occasion for this one was, and perhaps there was none. "I've smoked maybe two packs of cigarettes in my whole life, that's it."

WEIRA: "You wanted to know what significance this cigar held, but you were too nervous to ask?"

Whether it was a celebration.

WEIRA: "Or a detonation."

Is it either/or?

WEIRA: "Of course not."

It lent a mysteriously casual touch to the conversation. Therein another aspect of Pettibon: the fatal hand motion.

WEIRA: "*Forgetting the Hand*, as you recall."

It can't be forgotten, of course. Perhaps that's the joke. *No Title (For God's sake . . .)*, 1983: a woman has etched into her wrist:

FOR GOD'S SAKE HELP ME BEFORE I WRITE AGAIN!

WEIRA: "You've been there. But let's formulate a theory of the cigar and Ray: that it stood for nothing more than what it was, and in being itself—a casual cigar—it was something like a tweet, ever ready to commemorate or detonate at a moment's notice."

In 2011.

WEIRA: "In 2011, wasn't that what you drew you to it?"

What drew him to it, too. The big boom of Present Things.

WEIRA: "Speculation. Overruled. But yes, there was no ignoring its . . . incendiary . . . potential. Two things that hold true in Ray's work, two things that are well illustrated by my story of the Kaiser: the word and the bomb, both of which make and unmake one another, both of which are integral to Ray's art. There are always bombs going off in Ray's work, or rather there is one bomb, the bomb of history, which goes off in some place as soon as the dust has settled in another.

"The bomb was an almost inconceivable extension of dynamite (from the Greek word for 'power'), developed under different circumstances and for different purposes, and yet we might still trace it back to Nobel in his lab, cooking up easy death in Geesthacht in 1867. Within a year, the sticks were used in the Franco-German War of 1870 to '71 by the Germans, which ended with the German acquisition of Alsace-Lorraine—one of the direct causes of the First World War. And so, an arms race kicked off that led to the Manhattan Project. The bomb is always trying to stop the talking, to silence."

Real Political Thuygs dnt act for the cameras. They ACT-- in silence and in stealth.

2:45 PM – 21 Jan 2017

That was the day after you-know-who put his hand on the Bible at the Capitol's rear. Pettibon shouts to keep the silence from coming in:

Who I'm 4. Think abouyt it fooyls. 4 Self-Determination, Peace, Diplomacy. Against war, death, imperialism.

9:26 PM – 10 Mar 2016

There it is, at heart.

WEIRA: "Think abouyt it fooyls."

In a work from 2000, a woman screams:

THE SINGER NOT THE SONG!

WEIRA [*heading to the record player*]: "Oh yes. We are tearing our-selves apart!" [*The first bars of The Supremes' "I Hear a Symphony" begins to fill the room. The beast approaches THE WRITER and lifts him off his chair. They link arms and begin to shuffle awkwardly together.*]

A work from 1991 reads:

I GATHERED THOUGHTS, MEANINGS AND PRAYERS AT ONCE MORE BRIGHTLY TRANSPARENT, YET MORE FORMIDABLE THAN THE RUINS OF ILLUSTRIOUS CITIES HAD EVER CALLED UP TO ME.

DIANA ROSS: "I'm lost in a world made for you and me."

WEIRA: "Pfft. No more than a fuse. The biggest, bluest, bestest bomb — our earth."

No Title (And I believe . . .), 1995, written on a cloud:

AND I BELIEVE THE MORE THE READER REVOLVES THE SUBJECT IN HIS THOUGHTS, AND THE MORE OPPORTUNITIES HE HAS OF EXAMINING THE EXISTING FACTS, THE LESS EXPLICABLE THESE FACTS WILL BECOME TO HIM, AND THE MORE REVERENT WILL BE HIS ACKNOWLEDGMENT OF THE PRESENCE OF THE CLOUD.

DIANA ROSS: "Don't let this feeling end. Let it go on and on and on now, baby."

WEIRA [*singing along*]: "Baby, baby, those tears that fill my eyes,
I care not for myself but for those who've never felt the joy we've felt."

Cirrus, or cumulus? A chemtrail stretched at the horizon?

The page, for its part, is white.

Or cream.

A little stained.

Watermarks. The ink runs.

Another work from 1991 reads:

THE PAGES WHICH CONTAIN TRUTH ARE BLANK.

DIANA ROSS: "A thousand violins fill the air now. Baby, baby
don't let this moment end."

WEIRA [*whispering over the sound of the record*]: "Let me leave you
with this image, a last exposiyv shoyrt T: that of the widening cloud
that reduces all to dust and shadow. We are swirling in the black, writer.
Speak uyp. It's against this that our words must work. You follow? Do
you know my favorite of his drawings of the bomb? Its caption?"

[*The record stops.*]

Which?

WEIRA: "It says, 'How comes it so great a silence has fallen?'"

26

[RAYMOND PETTIBON *walks over to a filing cabinet near the kitchen.* THE
WRITER *joins him. He begins to rifle through over-stuffed drawers, searching
for a specific folder. He pulls out different ones, checks their subject, and then puts
them back. There seems to be little order to the cabinet, but whatever arrange-
ment there is, the artist is aware of the system that keeps things together. Finally,
he finds the one he's looking for and they return to the table. It is arguably the*

most important folder in the cabinet, THE WRITER *later learns.* RAYMOND PETTIBON *passes it over to him.*]

RAYMOND PETTIBON: "This is writing on the subject of the black square. Those go back many years and it's not, it's not something that . . . I may have done . . ."

[*The folder contains torn pages of books, handwritten notes, and xeroxes. On each, the artist has underlined sentences extensively, occasionally adding notes in the margin or between lines.*]

THE WRITER: "What's the black square?"

RAYMOND PETTIBON: "You know, Malevich or Reinhardt."

THE WRITER: "You scan these . . ."

RAYMOND PETTIBON: "Well those are just in my notes, but there's also maybe some . . . cut out from pages there somewhere."

THE WRITER: "I see. Do you mind if I pull this out?"

27

The folder is blue, somewhat damaged, its edges bent and worn down from years of use, from having been moved here and there and then shoved back among folders like it. Within it, there are smaller folders and envelopes containing hundreds, maybe thousands of strips of paper, each cut from different books and notebooks Pettibon has kept over the years. The strips represent threads of the artist's reading life: bits of novels, religious texts, histories, and poems. It is virtually impossible to tell, on sight, where many of them come from and what their original context might be. They read like fragments of parchment recovered from antiquity. I ask Pettibon if I can pull them out. He says yeah, sure.

I open the envelopes and folders. The slips of paper spill onto the table.

THE WRITER: "How long have you been keeping this?"

RAYMOND PETTIBON: "About thirty years."

Each slip, he tells me, relates in some way to the Reinhardtian black square: a painting, Reinhardt wrote, that "does not reflect its surroundings—a pure, abstract, non-objective, timeless, spaceless, changeless, relationless, disinterested painting—an object that is self-conscious (*no unconsciousness*), ideal, transcendent, aware of no thing but art (*absolutely no anti-art*)." As a reader, Pettibon scans for the presence of the black square in literature, and when he finds it, he draws a ■ next to the text. Like so:

■ one's life, the heterogeneous, miscellaneous apology for a Square marking the spot at which the main entrance, as ■

Sometimes, he marks off a phrase within a sentence, too:

■ sedative mood music. | I didn't know where we were going but sensed that a door had been opened that wouldn't easily close again. | ■
■ affections; for friendship maketh indeed a fair day in the affections from storm and tempests | but it maketh daylight in the understanding, out of darkness and confusion of thoughts: | neither is this to be ■
■ | Feeling rather faint she hurried through tunnels | made

I ask Pettibon if I can have some time alone with the folder. He nods and steps away to work on the screenplay while I head to a couch in front of a television in the back of the studio. I open each folder, notebook, sheet of paper, and envelope, carefully removing the notes and clippings he has assembled over the past three decades. I lay out the slips based on which envelope I find them in, but notice upon reading them that there is no organization to the folder, or at least not one recognizable to me. They are in a jumble, probably shoved into whatever envelope was at hand when Pettibon was cutting.

The black square is many things in Pettibon's reading of it. It is a supernaturally dark night, for example:

■ There is an evening coming in
Across the field, one never seen before,
That lights no lamps.

(Philip Larkin, I later discover.)

It is also a couch of vermillion leather, a painting of an "Arcadian youth that has never grown grey," it is "the bestial" that poetry strives to lift us out of. It is the false depth of a rhetorician's obscurity, which a crowd stands in awe of because "it cannot see the bottom." It is bottomlessness itself. It is "controllable windows." It is, in what I recognize to be Robert Louis Stevenson, the body that is "a house of many windows" in which the occupant lies "languishing, uncomforted, unchangeably alone." It is a black shirt. It is what is hidden from God. The black square is "some mysterious bureau" from which a man sallies forth onto boulevards. It is a tunnel. It is "under New York City," where an unknown woman goes. It is a "vision of the future."

In other instances, the black square's identifiable qualities are considerably vaguer. One enigmatic slip reads: "We use up too much artistry in our dreams—and therefore often are impoverished during the day." (Nietzsche, as it turns out.)

Also: "every stain so carefully scratched out"; "an oracle of inward life"; "He looked at the floor and pouted"; "These wanderers of the wastelands, like Dismukes and himself, were not laboring under fancy or blindness or ignorance or imagination or delusion. They were certainly not actuated by a feeling for some nameless thing. The desert was a fact" (Zane Grey); "the abounding page."

■ "in which all deficiencies will be made up."

■ A facsimile of a drawing by Pettibon (one of the very few images in the folder and the only one by him) that depicts a devil swinging a cross pendant.

90

On several of the larger, crinkled pages (drippy xeroxes of poems, mostly), Pettibon has made extensive notes or revisions to a found text. The word "author," for example, found in an essay of literary criticism, becomes, in his scribble, an "artist." Beneath a description of the evening colors of a mountain, he wrote "CROSSHATCHER," an apt metaphor for his work, which shades intersecting texts, histories, moods into a singular body of work.

Twiyt, twiyt.

Another slip: a short excerpt from Brad Gooch's biography of Frank O'Hara, *City Poet*—reads:

Her remark, and the visit, inspired O'Hara to write a poem originally titled "Ode at the Grave of Jackson Pollock," in which he asked Pollock for inspiration as if the Abstract Expressionist artist were a classical muse:

and like that child at your grave make me be distant and

imaginative

make my lines thin as ice, then swell like pythons

Between the lines of O'Hara's poem, Pettibon wrote:

■ They were serving black coffee (how even you'd like it as long as it's black) for the opening, and for as many second cups they were pouring, you know it had to be a great success.

The black square is a cup of coffee.

The black square is a flexible, freewheeling imaginative framework for the artist and, within it, Pettibon locates a vast psychological world, one consumed by dark or nocturnal mysteries, urban crawls, broken strands of literary conversation, eerie realities. It is also a negation of the world, and a port to the subaltern. Two handwritten pages expound on the black square in a sequence of "no" statements:

91

■ no cut, no stuff, no fouling out, no twist n' shout, no lay up, no
laid out.

Another, titled "Trade," begins with a meditation on Reinhardt but
moves, quickly, into a story of the art world personified as a fleeing
Madonna:

■ It is not rectangle, doubtless, but when was a square panorama.
Do like we do—another argument held against the edge—butt-
end two canvases end to butt-end, making one big ol' butt. It's
like seeing the end in cinemascope . . .

Pettibon's black square, including the fragmentary figures who
inhabit it, who emerge from it, and who disappear into it, is tracked
along with its inverse, the white square, which he notes on occasion in
the folder (along with the crucifix). But the white square seems, in the
end, to be less interesting to him, and examples of it are considerably
fewer: it is the light, of course, and openness, two qualities Pettibon
rarely treats in his work except in those instances where their supposed
goodness obscures a more menacing motive.

Pettibon walks over and joins me. He's holding the cigar. The
actors are loudly rehearsing the film script on the other end of the studio, but I can't make out any of the dialogue. One actor grows frustrated
when a call interrupts the reading. Sound ping-pongs off the walls in
muffled bursts. The actor and I make eye contact as she leaves to take
her call in the stairwell.

Pettibon doesn't say anything. He looks toward the door then
turns back to me.

I hold up the folder. This is a lot, I say.

RAYMOND PETTIBON: "You're looking at the black square or
rectangle. And that . . . for my . . . for my art, it's . . . [*long pause*] . . .
Speaking of Twitter, you only have so small a space to work in. And that

can be . . . poets . . . they can say the same thing . . . it's when you have a meager means of expression, that can be freedom at the same time. When you must rhyme, okay? When you have the rhyme and meter, it doesn't necessarily mean you're constricted to that. There's also . . . it can . . . it can help, you know, your expression. And with . . . the black rectangle, which is . . . Reinhardt finally got, you know, he did elements of color and rectangles and whatever and his . . . but he . . . he, he's also where I started, like comic books in a way, cartoons. Not so much comic books but cartoons. He was a brilliant writer. He . . . his writing illustrated his minimal . . . And so . . . all things you're pouring into . . . uh . . . Reinhardt . . . I'm taking, the, I'm making it literate, not literal. Starting with the black square, right? And, uh, I don't know, he'd be turning in his grave if he knew that. But I think he had this sense of humor to . . . to understand . . . there's literary and then there's literal. It's a big difference."

THE WRITER: "Can I show you a few things in here that I found? I would like you to respond to them, maybe you can say why they're here."

[THE WRITER *produces four panels of a Mexican comic book in which a couple embrace and are gradually consumed by the night surrounding them.* RAYMOND PETTIBON *considers this, then waits for the next image* THE WRITER *hands him. The second one is a cut out from a glossy magazine showing a scene from* The Graduate. *In it, Dustin Hoffman's character peers through a cocktail glass. The magazine captioned the film still: "Mirage."* RAYMOND PETTIBON *takes the image, turns it over, and remarks that he likes the film.*]

THE WRITER: "What about the second one."

RAYMOND PETTIBON: "It's with a white square. I'm trying to think . . . why?"

THE WRITER: "It says 'mirage'? So, in the glass, it appears that there's a crucifix—a perfect synthesis of the folder, really, given it mixes the white square—the glass; the black square—the shadow in the glass; and the crucifix—formed inside both."

RAYMOND PETTTIBON: "Oh, okay. Perhaps. I'm trying to figure it out myself. Maybe I was thinking the glass would be a white rectangle itself. Reflecting, reflective. From Malevich to Albers to . . . the black rectangle or the white is such a part of art history. The point was to bleed basically, to make it just, uh, to bleed all the literary out of it. The whole point of my thing was to start with the most minimal black or white image and then to make it purple . . . you know . . . in language . . . purple prose, the literary. And that was, at the time, that was, you couldn't do that. I'm not the first person to add language to, uh, the most, the paucity of . . . forms, but that was the point, okay? I love Reinhardt's writing, his poetry, his prose. But I'm doing the opposite . . . well, I don't know . . . he's been dead for so many years and I don't owe him anything."

THE WRITER: "He feels like a forerunner?"

RAYMOND PETTIBON: "In some ways. I'm breaking the rules. But what the fuck. What rules? Who gives a fuck? If you read art criticism of, you know, the sixties or seventies, it's hard to . . . it's hard to keep on topic. Although, it's not like I'm making some critique of it or whatever. I'm using, in this case, the black square or rectangle as a starting point to . . . to write. I'm not Robert Ryman who can recreate the white square endlessly. I'm not a great artist. Let's be honest, that's figurative art, when you do a white ass or a black rectangle, it's a starting point, it's a subject matter . . . and to go off on it lyrically, okay, my art work is about writing and lyrical writing and that can start with a paucity of means, you know. It could be anything. I always thought I could take a grain of dirt and write on the subject and do something with it."

28

Hundreds of strips of paper surround me, in piles and clumps arrayed across the small couch, and their different shapes and typefaces tumble together with longer, typed pages of quotes that Pettibon has assembled over the years: "movable dirt," as he writes in one note in the folder. I consider this phrase, "over the years," and decide whether to flag it for later revision, maybe even excision, since I am not sure I fully understand the way time works for Pettibon. The phrase might be rewritten as "gradually assembled," "accrued," "built-up" since he works by slow accumulation, like a stalagmite rises from a ceiling's drypdrypdrypings over thousands of years. The years accumulate, of course, fall upon one another, move in a sequence. But Pettibon doesn't work sequentially; rather, his inquiries—the crucifix, the white square, and the black square, to name three formations in one of his caves—seem to progress slowly, in scattershot periods of reading. There are no years, there are readings, which take place over much lengthier, spun-out periods of time. Pettibon's a rock, growing slowly ever larger.

I review the strips while Pettibon finishes the cigar.

He looked at the floor and pouted (■). | How clear had been his vision | (■) but because God's word has been said to thee, | I can conceal naught from Him to whom nothing is hidden. (■) | realizing to such a degree | we often find in his foregrounds rich masses of colour, of light and of shade, which, when examined, mean nothing | (■). In Titian, there is equal breath, equal sub-whelming, had been | the form of vigilance posting itself (■) | at the window |—whence, incontestably, after a little, completely blind for his final twenty years, <u>we are confronted</u> in Paradise Lost by <u>an oracle of the inward life.</u> (■) No more deliberate masterpiece ex- | and a multitude of fantastical lines that go to make a dead wall (■) of paint after ten years' work. | Neither were Rolfe's manuscript pages 'covered with illegible boneless scribblings' as were those papers that he had discovered in his coat pocket, (■) | with the result, Stevens recalls, that 'there was snickering and laughing and most of the women in the group were about ready to climb out the window. (■) It was all kept so dark, | every stain so carefully scratched out, (■) every whisper so swiftly choked | that whereas I now have to refuse | Who knows what hearts and souls have in them (■) |

on the train stuff, this travel from country to country. | Then you have to paint in this vast panorama full of precise details. (■) Why not make everything happen in your apartment? alluringly. It was what Adam had expected. It was what he wanted for her. | How clear had been his vision (■) | of the future! (■) | Feeling rather faint she hurried through tunnels | made conception, identified with the Holy Spirit of Christian doctrine, | and ~~wind~~ <black on canvas> is a concrete illustration of it. | But in the Greek text the same word, pneuma, is used for both wind and spirit. Hence a purely In Paris my most valued friend was a Frenchman, Maurice Cremnitz. (■) | Employed nobody knew how during the day, in the evening he would emerge from some mysterious bureau and sally forth on boulevards. His familiarity with (■) | moving to the Planet of the Archbuilders | real, inflating (■) | it to fill the space that had gaped | when Clement lost the (■) | I closed my eyes, leaned against the wall. |

The language pours forth, in bits and pieces. I push the slips about, trying to find my own order for them, but none emerges, or none that feels right. There is no rightness to the folder; rather, it sits in opposition to such an idea. The slips are like captions to drawings, too, and in this his drawings are themselves like tweets, or proto-tweets. It all begins here, in the folder (and likely among other folders, too, with other subjects and other notes), the work and the tweets, and the difference between them feels negligible. Pettibon has been tweeting his whole life, only for an audience of one. As a reader, he has been cutting things down to size, condensing moments and passages and poems and stories and arguments and fictions into fragments, each roughly 140 characters long, for decades.

I say, "Ray, these are like tweets. The papers."

He shrugs his shoulders. They are what they are, his face says. That is, his face says nothing. I put things back.

Acknowledgments

My gratitude to Raymond Pettibon for his kindness and his openness to all my questions as I rifled through his things. Shiv Kotecha and Lynne Tillman read early drafts of this manuscript, and I'd be nowhere without their sound advice and indispensable love. And thank you to my generous editor, Lucas Zwirner.

Further Resources

Raymond Pettibon: A Pen of All Work, ed. Massimiliano Gioni and Gary Carrion-Murayari. New York: Phaidon, 2017.

Raymond Pettibon: Homo Americanus, ed. Ulrich Loock and Harald Falckenberg. New York: David Zwirner Books, 2016.

Raymond Pettibon, Marcel Dzama, and Andrew Durbin, *Dzama/Pettibon,* 2nd ed. New York: David Zwirner Books, 2016. Accompanied the exhibition, *Forgetting the Hand*, David Zwirner, New York, January 14 – February 20, 2016.

Raymond Pettibon, ed. Ralph Rugoff. New York: Rizzoli, 2013.

W. G. Sebald, "Death Draws Nigh, Time Marches On," in *A Place in the Country*, trans. Jo Catling. New York: Random House, 2013.

Catherine Crowe, "A Story of a Weir-Wolf," *Hogg's Weekly Instructor*, May 16, 1847.

Marcel Proust, *In Search of Lost Time: Volume 3, The Guermantes Way* (1920–21), trans. Mark Traherne. New York: Penguin, 2005.

Benjamin H. D. Buchloh, "After Laughter," *October*, Summer 2009, pp. 13–50.

David Bowie, "Life on Mars," track 4 on *Hunky Dory*, RCA Records, 1971.

David Bowie, "The Supermen," track 9 on *The Man Who Sold the World*, Mercury Records, 1970.

David Bowie, "Big Brother," track 10 on *Diamond Dogs*, RCA Records, 1974.

Samuel Beckett, *Krapp's Last Tape and Embers.* London: Faber and Faber, 1958.

Sonic Youth, *Goo*, DGC Records, 1990.

Tattletales. Aired 1974–84, on CBS.

The Twilight Zone, Season 1, episode 33, "Mr. Bevis." Aired June 3, 1960, on CBS.

Frank Miller, *The Dark Night Rises.* New York: DC Comics, 1986.

Mary Shelley, *Frankenstein: The 1818 Text*, ed. Marilyn Butler.
Oxford: Oxford University Press, 2009.

Gustave Flaubert, *Madame Bovary* (1856), trans. Lydia Davis.
New York: Viking, 2010.

Janet Malcolm, *The Silent Woman: Sylvia Plath and Ted Hughes*.
New York: Knopf, 1994.

Jorge Luis Borges, "The Aleph" (1945) in *The Aleph and Other Stories*,
trans. Andrew Hurley. New York: Penguin Classics, 2004.

Ludwig Wittgenstein, *Tractatus Logico-Philosophicus* (1921),
trans. C. K. Ogden. London: Routledge & Kegan Paul, 1922.

Ad Reinhardt, *No War,* in *Artists and Writers Protest Against the War in Viet
Nam,* 1967. Lithograph, 66.2×53 cm.

Joachim Kalka, *Gaslight: Lantern Slides from the Nineteenth Century*,
trans. Isabel Fargo Cole. New York: New York Review of Books, 2017.

The Supremes, "I Hear a Symphony," track 3 on *I Hear a Symphony*,
Motown, 1965.

Philip Larkin, "Going" (1946), in *The Collected Poems*.
New York: Farrar Straus and Giroux, 2001.

Robert Louis Stevenson, "Virginibus Puerisque," in *Virginibus Puerisque
and Other Papers*. London: Chatto & Windus, 1897.

Zane Grey, *Wanderer of the Wasteland* (1923). New York:
HarperCollins, 1990.

Brad Gooch, *City Poet: The Life and Times of Frank O'Hara*.
New York: Harper Perennial, 1993.

List of Works

p. 13
No Title (So occasional, so . . .), 1992
Ink on paper, 14 × 10.75 inches
(35.5 × 27.3 cm)
Courtesy of Robert Berman
Gallery, Santa Monica, CA

p. 14
No Title (The singer not . . .), 2000
Pen and ink on paper,
22 ¼ × 16 inches (56.5 × 40.6 cm)
Courtesy David Zwirner, New York
Photo by: Dawn Blackman

p. 16
No Title (And I believe . . .), 1995
Pen and ink on paper,
8 ½ × 19 ½ inches (21.6 × 49.5 cm)
Courtesy David Zwirner, New York
Photo by: Dawn Blackman

p. 17
No Title (When they meet . . .), 2001
Ink on paper, 13 ½ × 19 ¾ inches
(34.3 × 50.2 cm)
Collection of David Weber,
Los Angeles
Courtesy David Zwirner, New York

p. 19
No Title (Which side of . . .), 1982
Pen and ink on paper,
11 × 8 ½ inches (27.9 × 21.6 cm)
Courtesy David Zwirner, New York
Photo by: Adam Reich

p. 20
No Title (Baltic Blue. The . . .), 2014
Ink, acrylic, gouache, and collage
on paper, 34 ½ × 56 inches
(87.6 × 142.2 cm)
Courtesy David Zwirner, New York
Photo by: Adam Reich

p. 21
No Title (Double Self-Portrait . . .), 1990
Pen and ink on paper,
22 × 17 inches (55.9 × 43.2 cm)
Collection of Alan Hergott
and Curt Shepard
Courtesy Regen Projects,
Los Angeles

p. 22
No Title (Our hero's alcoholism . . .),
1987
Ink on paper, 24 × 19 inches
(61.0 × 48.3 cm)
Private collection
Courtesy Blondeau & Cie, Geneva

p. 23
No Title (Of a bow . . .), 1991
Ink on paper, 22 × 20.325 inches
(55.9 × 51.6 cm)
Courtesy of Robert Berman
Gallery, Santa Monica, CA

p. 24
No Title (Life at these . . .), 1989
Pen and ink on paper,
14 × 11 inches (35.6 × 27.9 cm)
Courtesy Regen Projects,
Los Angeles

p. 25
No Title (Talking to myself . . .), 2014
Ink, acrylic, and pencil on paper,
19 × 24 inches (48.3 × 61 cm)
Courtesy David Zwirner, New York
Photo by: Jean Vong

p. 26
No Title (I love honest . . .), 2017
Ink and collage on paper,
30 ½ × 49 ½ inches
(77.5 × 125.7 cm)
Courtesy David Zwirner, New York
Photo by: Dan Bradica

p. 28
No Title (Faithful to truth . . .), 1998
Pen and ink on paper,
15 ⅜ × 11 ½ inches (39.1 × 29.2 cm)
Courtesy David Zwirner, New York
Photo by: Dan Bradica

p. 29
No Title (Then he began . . .), 1990
Pen and ink on paper,
22 × 17 inches (55.9 × 43.2 cm)
Courtesy David Zwirner, New York
Photo by: Dan Bradica

p. 30
Marcel Dzama
and Raymond Pettibon
The Supermen would walk in flames,
2016
Pencil, ink, watercolor, gouache,
acrylic, and collage on paper,
29 × 39 ¾ inches (73.7 × 101 cm)
Private collection, Portugal
Courtesy David Zwirner, New York
Photo by: Jean Vong

p. 31
Marcel Dzama
and Raymond Pettibon
Beware Diamond Dog, 2016
Pencil, ink, watercolor, gouache,
acrylic, pencil crayon, and collage
on paper and piano scroll,
36 ¾ × 24 ⅞ inches (93.3 × 63.2 cm)
Collection of Scott and
Margot Ziegler
Courtesy David Zwirner, New York
Photo by: Cooper Dodds

p. 32
No title (To the confounding . . .), 2002
Pen and ink on paper,
15 ¾ × 11 inches (40 × 27.9 cm)
Courtesy Regen Projects,
Los Angeles

Spiyt th'Words

Rereading Pettibon's Twitter

Published by

David Zwirner Books

529 W 20th St, 2nd Floor

New York, New York 10011

+1 212 727 2070

davidzwirnerbooks.com

Editor Lucas Zwirner

Project Manager Mary Huber

Copy Editor Dorothy Feaver

Designer Sarah Schrauwen

Production Manager Jules Thomson

Color Separations VeronaLibri, Verona

Printing VeronaLibri, Verona

Typefaces Larsseit, Swift Neue

Paper PlanoPlus 120 gsm

Publication

© **2018 David Zwirner Books**

Essay

© **2018 Andrew Durbin**

Artwork pp. 2, 6, 8, 10–14, 17, 19–26, 28–29, 32, 34

© **2018 Raymond Pettibon**

Artwork pp. 7, 30, 31

© **2018 Marcel Dzama and Raymond Pettibon**

Distributed in the United States and Canada by

ARTBOOK | D.A.P.

75 Broad Street, Suite 630

New York, New York 10004

artbook.com

Distributed outside the United States and Canada by

Thames & Hudson, Ltd.

181A High Holborn

London WC1V 7QX

thamesandhudson.com

ISBN 978-1-941701-75-1

LCCN 2018936730

Printed in Italy